THE CLASSIC WESTERN RIDER

DONNA SNYDER-SMITH

Cartoons by Dana Bauer

Howell
Book House™

THE CLASSIC WESTERN RIDER

DONNA SNYDER-SMITH

Cartoons by Dana Bauer

HB Howell
Book House™

Copyright © 2006 by Wiley Publishing, Inc., Hoboken, New Jersey. All rights reserved.

Illustrations copyright © 2006 by Dana Bauer.

Howell Book House
Published by Wiley Publishing, Inc., Hoboken, New Jersey

For general information on our other products and services or to obtain technical support please contact our Customer Care Department within the U.S. at (800) 762-2974, outside the U.S. at (317) 572-3993 or fax (317) 572-4002.

Wiley also publishes its books in a variety of electronic formats. Some content that appears in print may not be available in electronic books. For more information about Wiley products, please visit our web site at www.wiley.com.

Library of Congress Cataloging-in-Publication Data:
Snyder-Smith, Donna.
  Classic western rider / Donna Snyder-Smith.
    p. cm.
  ISBN-13: 978-0-7645-9920-0
  ISBN-10: 0-7645-9920-8
  1. Western riding. 2. Western horses—Training I. Title.
  SF309.3.S69 2006
  798.2'3—dc22

                              2006002965

Printed in the United States of America

10 9 8 7 6 5 4 3 2 1

Cover design by Wendy Mount
Book production by Wiley Publishing, Inc. Composition Services
Cartoons by Dana Bauer

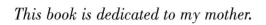

This book is dedicated to my mother.

Contents

Preface

To be or beat the best, you must learn from the best. This is not an easy task, because true masters seldom announce themselves, and there are many pretenders to the throne. Money can be helpful in your search for excellence, but cost alone doesn't define quality, so if you want to rise to the top, you must shoulder the responsibility of educating yourself. In order to acquire excellence, you must first acquire the ability to *recognize* excellence. Further, you must be an active seeker, not satisfied to wait on your doorstep for that which you need to seek *you* out.

Introduction

Whether you're a new rider interested in the western style of riding; an intermediate rider who wishes to polish specific performance skills in a discipline such as western horsemanship; an amateur adult rider looking for new thrills on the back of a sleek, catty, reining horse; or an experienced competitor on the lookout for that special riding or training tip that can help you get a better performance from your horse, *The Classic Western Rider* has something to offer.

If you're new to horses and/or western riding, you'll appreciate the glossary at the back of this book, with its clear and simple explanation of the many terms used in the western riding vocabulary. While meaningful to those more experienced in the world of horses and western horsemanship, these terms can leave beginners in a fog as they try to figure out the meaning of words such as roll back, reiner, hand, and hackamore.

Chapter 1 explores the cowboy lifestyle and the influence of Hollywood on the shaping of the cowboy legend, including little-known facts about both real-life and silver-screen cowboys and their horses.

It's easy to buy a saddle, and nearly everyone who owns a horse does it, but it takes experience to learn the nuances that separate a good saddle from an average one. Although the important topic of saddle fit as it relates to horse and rider performance has received some exposure in industry magazines in recent years, chapter 2 offers another extremely important level of knowledge, with a look at how training and the carriage of a horse influences the horse's musculature and saddle fit on an ongoing basis.

Although it's impossible to cover everything about training horses in one book, chapter 3 offers you a navigation system: a map to the experience. Like any good navigation system, the chapter gives you an overview of the best, most direct route to your desired destination. This information includes important references to where to find additional fuel (information), alerts you to signs signaling a potential hazard, and gives you an estimation of the travel time between important points or events you are likely to encounter during your journey.

Being a partnership, riding has a lot in common with dancing. Chapter 4 gives you essential tips on how to avoid stumbling over your partner's feet, and teaches some basic lessons in the footwork that will allow you to stand out on the dance floor by expressing your own style gracefully, with confident skill.

On the topic of style, whether you favor the natural western look or enjoy the glitter and glamour of the attire seen in today's show arena, chapter 5 is packed with fashion tips and essential information on the cowboy costume. There is also an insider's look at what goes into the making of the cowboy hat, the most recognizable symbol of the western rider.

Then jog into chapter 6 to benefit from the advice of a veteran equitation coach. Learn the secrets of what it takes to win in the western horsemanship class in the highly competitive world of the show ring.

Reining is one of the fastest-growing western events around the world, and the first western event recognized by the Federation Equestrian International, the equestrian body that recognizes and governs all Olympic equestrian disciplines. Chapter 7 offers critical advice that may not only lead to enjoying the event but may prevent injury to both rider and horse during this high-powered, stylized form of "horse ballet."

If you are more the type who feels a real need for speed when you're on the back of a horse, you will enjoy reading about the western skills contests described in chapters 8 and 9, which include training tips from a champion competitor on how to best prepare your horse to win at these challenging tests of speed and maneuverability.

Chapter 1

Classic Western Riding: History and Hollywood

Go Ahead, Make My Day

If English riding can be labeled as elegant, a pursuit of kings, nobles, and the upper classes, western riding can be said to be tough, the choice of working-class men and women. While western riding as we know it today may have had its roots in the riding traditions of both Spain and Mexico, once those traditions crossed the border into the United States, they became inexorably shaped by the men and women of the west and southwest, who lived out much of their lives aboard a horse's back. Today's western traditions have also been shaped by the literary world and by Hollywood. Like it or not, today's image of the cowboy and his gear has been influenced as much by the early dime novels, Hollywood movies, and television as it ever was by any cowhand who walked the streets of El Paso or helped to turn a herd of stampeding cattle.

The History of the Cowboy

The cowboy tradition is so strong that it survived a lengthy period when horses as working tools were virtually obsolete, abandoned in favor of trucks and tractors. So what elements make up this mysterious, historical, legendary persona that continues to influence so many of today's riders?

Historical records would seem to indicate that the "boy" part of the term was appropriate. Documents and photographs suggest that the earliest members of this particular social group were, in fact, *boys*, ranging in age from thirteen or fourteen into their early twenties. Historians have postulated that many in the group were orphans or the fatherless sons of men who died during our country's Civil War. As a group, they were generally poorly educated, most having limited reading or writing skills. They were also "minimum wage" employees of the time. Their job consisted of working with stock, whether on a ranch or the open range. Working conditions were often harsh, the hours were long, and the work was hard and dirty. There was little in the way of comfort and almost no promise of advancement either in wages or in social position. Some have argued that the men who answered to the title "cowboy" in its earliest appearance on the world stage were men of little significance. Yet ironically, while factual history may uphold that particular point of view, the myths that arose around this group of men have caused the figure of the cowboy to surpass all other legendary figures, in both reality and fiction, in their ability to influence multiple generations.

The King Ranch, Volume I, maintains that the name "cow-boys" originally appeared on the historical landscape as a descriptive term for gangs of young toughs who daringly rode into Mexico to steal cattle, driving them north to sell to U.S. government agents, buying beef for federal troops located north of the Nueces line in Texas. In light of today's rap and hip-hop lyrics that tell hard-edged stories of gang life, it is interesting to note that one of our country's most revered icons, the American cowboy, also originated in a gang environment. These boys drifted from job to job throughout much of the country west of the Mississippi River, from Montana to Texas and westward to California. Whether this gypsy tendency was inherent in their psychological and emotional makeup or was forced upon them by the lack of stability in their particular job market is speculative. Similarities to today's gangs included their reputation for substance abuse (alcohol), gambling, and their rowdy, sometimes destructive behavior. They tended to mistrust authority and shunned the company of merchants, bankers, lawmen, set-tlers, and farmers. While Hollywood would later dress their manners in a more chivalrous style, early historical accounts of gunplay and drunken brawling suggest otherwise. It is fair to assume that these young men, like gangs today, found a sense of family within their ranks, and this circumstantial family may have had a strong influence on an indi-vidual member's behavior. But it is likely these acquired family mem-bers would judge, accept, or reject a man based on his present qualities and qualifications, rather than on his past history, a fact that allowed a "loner" to fit in.

In *Cowboys of the Old West: The Real Face of the American Cowboy*, William Forbis writes, "neither flash impressions nor bare statistics can take the true measure of the cowboys or dim the elemental stage pres-ence and the riveting appeal they generated in their own time and for-ever afterward. They were men of a particular time and place, living by a code compounded of hard fisted frontier desperation and Victorian-era social values, performing body-punishing and hazardous jobs, and pit-ting themselves against a land of sweeping grandeur that offered prodi-gious drafts of misery!"

The Partnership of Horse and Man

From the beginning, a cowboy thought of his horse as a tool of the trade. That is not to say these men didn't appreciate a fine-quality tool. Such a tool made life easier, and there is an inherent pres-tige in owning quality tools, as any good carpenter, electrician, or mechanic will tell you. However, not all men (or women) who sit upon a horse are true horsemen.

The horseman perceives his or her horse as an equal and realizes the horse is both a partner and a critically important teammate, one on whom the rider's life may well depend. Understanding that partner and being able to afford them the courtesy of clear com-munication was not a common subject of books in the early history of the west, but a horseman was identifiable by demonstration, in the way he sat his horse, and in the way the pair performed their job. Such a connection between man and horse was visible even to an undiscerning eye and admired by all of the contemporaries of such a pair.

East

West

Standing alone in one's choices is difficult. The backbone it requires is a trait that is often credited to the legendary cowboy.

The modern-day expression "cowboy up" is an admonition to look outward, away from the needs of self to the needs of the group, or a job that wants doing. In a world often focused on the self, it is a strong dose of reality, which says the tough not only survive but are often the shapers of the future. "Tough" in the cowboy context has much greater inclusion than mere physical prowess, displayed in muscular strength or in the ability to withstand discomfort and pain. Today, the word "tough" as relates to the cowboy persona has come to imply a moral benchmark, one that indicates a man or woman can be counted on to stand by his or her beliefs. Its implied reference to a standard is built upon the emotional resilience that enables those who possess it to withstand the debilitating psychological effects of close proximity to death. The power this attribute conveys springs only from a blending of toughness and mercy, and gives those who possess the quality an ability to destroy, by their own hand, something loved, rather than taking the easy way out by leaving the job in the hands of a stranger or nature. A difficult act of destruction, motivated by true benevolence, brings someone as close to godhood as he or she may be while still alive. This was an act that a cowboy, given the circumstances of his environment and time, could be called upon to perform more than once in a lifetime.

The Cowboy Persona

Whether you find yourself riding a western saddle or an English one could be a simple result of your geographical location, or it could be influenced by the jobs you want to accomplish or, in the show world, the classes you want to participate in with your horse. But your choice could also represent a desire to possess those qualities you associate with what you perceive to be the persona of others who have chosen similarly.

In the present, where convenience and frustration hold almost equal sway over our lives, it is fair to ask if the man or woman who rides a western saddle isn't, at some level, attempting to navigate through life by the simple truths that served the men and women who wore a similar

The Very First Life-Skills Course?

Today, emotionally troubled children, as well as adults, can enroll in survival courses today in order to discover their ability to overcome their fears by surviving hardships. Perhaps the young men who pitted themselves against nature, the land, hunger, thirst, sickness, and injury to make their living as cowboys were the first-generation participants in a vast and very real survival course, one whose lesson of self-worth through self reliance is passed down, along with their fashions, to today's western riders.

uniform in the past. Watching a rider in a western pleasure class sporting rhinestone-studded collar and cuffs and riding a light-colored saddle bedecked with silver, it can be hard to imagine the dust-covered, half-baked or half-frozen trail hand who doggedly moved cattle across vast plains or through treacherously swollen rivers and over mountain passes, who roped, doctored, branded, and babied the animals that have played such a large role in the economic history of the country. Yet at some level, the show ring rider does indeed consider himself or herself connected to that historical figure, and unconsciously hopes to command the respect now accorded its original titleholder.

The Influence of Popular Media

The cowboy persona, whether legend or fact, cannot be seriously defined without examining the impact of the fertile minds of early dime novelists such as Ned Buntline. Cheap and sensationalistic novels were a part of the American landscape as far back as 1860; however, not until Owen Wister wrote his best-selling novel, *The Virginian, Horseman of the Plains*, were cowboys painted as loners with a strict code of honor.

Movies

Actors first began to contribute their representations of the American cowboy not in movies but rather in the very popular Wild West shows, such as *Buffalo Bill's Wild West*, and the *101 Ranch Real Wild West* show. Later, Hollywood and television would further shape the public's imagination about the historical figure of the cowboy, when the work of various authors was made real through the acting skills of flesh-and-blood men such as John Wayne (*Stagecoach* and *True Grit*), Gary Cooper (*High Noon*), Gregory Peck (*The Gunfighter*), Henry Fonda (*My Darling Clementine*), Jimmy Stewart (*The Man From Laramie*), and Kirk Douglas (*Lonely Are the Brave*). Such men forever imprinted the persona of the American cowboy on the minds and hearts of their millions of fans and viewers.

When you put on a western hat and boots, have you ever caught yourself changing your behavior, even just a little, taking on the traits or mannerisms of the traditional figure? In evaluating the importance of the impact of that unique and mysterious figure known as the cowboy, it needs to be remembered that even though the above-named actors played a variety of roles during their careers, many become most closely identified with and best remembered for their roles in westerns. John Wayne, an American icon, earned his superstar status by depicting the western leading man as tough, unflinchingly honest, willing and able to stand up for what he believed in, and equally at home on a horse's back or in a barroom brawl. Yet he also preached temperance of force, often using humor rather than physical strength to disarm and gain an advantage. (Watching his movies, I have more than once caught myself wondering how much of that particular style of problem solving lay with the scriptwriter or director of the picture, and how much came from the Duke himself!) If you're a part of the younger generation and haven't yet gone retro, your list of western roles models might include Clint Eastwood (*Unforgiven, The Magnificent Seven,* and *The Good, the Bad and the Ugly*), Paul Newman and Robert Redford (*Butch Cassidy and the Sundance Kid*), or Kevin Costner (*Silverado, Dances with Wolves,* and *Open Range*).

Ever think your choice of saddle and style of riding could reveal facets of your inner self or lock you into a way of responding to the world? In the movie *The Misfits,* Clark Gable gives the audience a fascinating look at the war raging within his cowboy character, a man caught in a trap of expectations, both his own and others', and unable to live his life to the standard he has inherited with his title. Classic westerns such as *Shane* and *High Noon* also showed men in moral conundrums, each one struggling to live up to a code they seemed to have inherited along with the hat. The writers of these stories, and the men who enacted their vision, believed in the far-reaching power of the title "cowboy," and the power that image carried, to shape the lives of the men who claimed it.

Television

Western TV series, such as *The Virginian, Gunsmoke, The Rifleman, Have Gun Will Travel,* and *Bonanza,* also contributed lifelong templates of the western man to a generation of young viewers. As adults, these viewers would push the Nielsen ratings of miniseries such as *Lonesome Dove* and *Legends of the Fall* through the roof.

Singing Cowboys

All of the men who starred in various westerns portrayed the cowboy as tough, independent, and resourceful, as well as associating him with a particular saddle and style of riding. But the true prophets of the sweeping reform in horse-handling techniques taking place in the United States today were Roy Rogers and Gene Autry—men who would be referred to by western historians (sometimes disdainfully) as "singing cowboys"—and before them, a writer and illustrator named Will James.

In the early 1900s, Will James wrote and illustrated more than sixteen books about cowboys and the horses that were a part of their lives. Two of his best-known and -loved titles were *Smokey, the Cow Horse* (first published in 1926 by Charles Scribner's Sons) and *Lone Cowboy.* In the preface of *Smokey,* James clearly reveals his position on the relationship between the horse and the man who rode him:

> I've never yet went wrong in sizing up a man by the kind of
> a horse he rode. A good horse always packs a good man. My
> life, from the time I first squinted at daylight, has been with
> horses. I admire every step that creature makes. I know them
> and been thru so much with 'em that I've come to figger a big
> mistake was made when the horse was classed as an animal.
> To me, the horse is man's greatest, most useful, faithful, and
> powerful friend. He never whines when he's hungry or sore
> footed or tired, and he'll keep on a going for the human till
> he drops.

Through their movies, television shows, and comic books, horse lovers Gene Autry and Roy Rogers continued this same concept—that is, the horse as more than a necessary piece of the cowboy's equipment, to be mastered and used in his job, like his rifle or his rope. Before these men, if a cowboy's horse was given any attention at all by writers or by Hollywood, it was as an ornament to the stories of the obstacles a man had to surmount in claiming the title. Horses were "broken" to saddle, used hard, and depicted as worthy of no more consideration than being tied to a hitching rack and left standing for hours under the hot sun while their rider drank or gambled at the town's saloon. Occasionally one might see a horse being watered or stabled at the local livery stable when the cowboy hero rode in to a town, but the men who played these lead roles projected no love of the animal. That would change radically with the entrance of both Roy Rogers and Gene Autry, whose horses, Trigger and Champion, would become so well known to readers and viewers that they would eventually be the featured stars in their own line of comic books.

One of the most radical changes the story lines these men both employed was to feature their horses as intelligent partners, often giving them input to the story by counting on them to rescue someone from danger. At other times, Trigger and Champion were relied on for their unerring, almost mystical instincts about good versus evil.

These equine actors responded to a great range of verbal and visual commands (much like a trained dog), were depicted as being able to make decisions on their own, and were treated with great respect and love; viewed by both men as partners and as friends.

Trigger and Champion, comic book stars.

Gene Autry had ridden horses in his childhood, while Roy
Rogers (shown in the photo on the following page) didn't
hone his riding skills until he became involved in acting. In
her book *Cowboy Princess,* Roy's daughter Cheryl Rogers-
Barnett tells the story of her father and Trigger: Trigger had
more than a little to do with helping Dad acquire this riding
skills. Dad worked with some great stuntmen and wranglers.
He was what they call a "quick study" and it didn't take him
long to pick out the horsemen who he thought rode best and
then to figure the mechanics of what they were doing that he
liked. He then set himself the task of copying what they
were doing. Dad and Trigger would work together for hours
on end until they could anticipate the other's demands.

Rogers apparently liked to credit his horse with playing an important
part in his success:

Dad loved to tell the story of how the studio head came to
him when Dad was trying to negotiate a raise in his contract,
and in essence told him, 'Thanks, but no thanks. We can put
anybody on Trigger!'
Dad replied, 'No, you can't put anybody on Trigger—he's
my horse, I'm buying him!' and he really was. Almost from
the minute Dad laid eyes on Trigger, he knew that horse was
something very, very special, so even though he didn't make
much money, he decided to buy the four year old stallion
from his owners, Hudkins Brothers. Dad and Ace Hudkins
stuck up a deal for Roy to make payment while Ace continued
to rent Trigger to Republic (Pictures), but he wouldn't let
them put another cowboy on him—until the last payment
had been made. It took a couple of years for Roy to make all
the payments—after all, he was making $75 a week, and he
paid $2,500 for that horse!

The original Trigger was sired by a thoroughbred and out of a quarter
horse mare, and co-starred in all eighty-two movies made by Roy Rogers
between 1938 and 1952. He also appeared in all one hundred TV
episodes of *The Roy Rogers Show.* Gene Autry's horse, the original
Champion, was a Tennessee Walker. Champion achieved so much fame

that he wound up with his own TV series, *The Adventures of Champion,* which ran on CBS for twenty-six episodes, from 1955 to 1956. Gene Autry claimed he paid only $1,500 for his famous horse.

That both men loved their equine co-stars was evident in their work with them in movies, television, and personal appearances. One might go so far as to wonder if the sensitivity this new type of cowboy hero displayed in his relationship with his equine companion(s) was at least partially responsible for the adoration of their millions of fans. That it was the most visible early indicator of today's changing views of the role the horse plays in the picture of the western cowboy is without argument.

Roy Rogers, king of the cowboys.

In keeping with this more refined, fancier garbed version of the American cowboy (the clothing worn by riders in the pleasure and equitation divisions today is a direct design offshoot of the colorful, stylish type of clothing sported by the singing cowboys), Gene Autry and Roy Rogers downplayed violence and promoted kindness and fair treatment of both horses and their fellow man in their movies, TV series, and comic books. While simplistic in the story lines, this kinder, gentler approach to the American icon brought huge popularity and success to both men. This author believes it also set in motion a tiny pebble of perception about horses. That pebble has been rolling downhill and gaining momentum and magnitude ever since, until today we are witnessing an avalanche of awareness (promoted by the cowboy horse-whisperer clinicians and their kinder, gentler methods of training and communication) whose effects change for the better the lives of millions of people and their horses.

Chapter 2

Saddle Savvy:
The Tools of Your Trade

Saddle Construction

While you don't need to know as much about how a saddle is constructed as a saddle maker does, you do need enough information to make an informed choice when it comes to your most important piece of equipment and what could easily be a very big-ticket item. Most western saddles are built around a *saddletree* (as shown in the photo on the following page). All old western saddles as well as some current models have carved, laminated wood trees, which have been wrapped in wet rawhide, which has been laced or nailed into place, and then allowed to dry, shrinking to fit in the process, and giving the saddle its strength and flexibility.

Newer western models—especially lightweight, inexpensive, and synthetic models—often have fiberglass or aluminum trees. While fiberglass and aluminum trees are lighter in weight than their wooden

No horn?

Equipment must meet the needs of the job but best serves when it offers both security and comfort as well.

cousins, experts will argue that rawhide-covered wood has more flexibility. However, if the weight of your saddle is your greatest concern, modern materials can meet your needs.

Someone who rides *rough stock*—young, unbroken colts or rank, older problem horses who are likely to buck with a rider—will benefit from riding in a *swell-forked, high-cantle saddle* because these features add to the rider's security. The roper, however, will want to choose an *A* or *slick fork saddle* with a low cantle. Cutting horse riders—whose horses must make extremely fast, successive, athletic movements when cutting out a cow from a herd or preventing one from returning to the herd—require a saddle with a level, balanced seat. Those who ride in western pleasure and equitation classes in the show ring usually chose a seat that rises toward the fork, stabilizing their seat against the cantle.

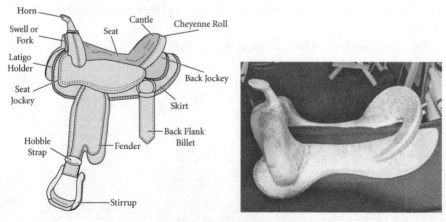

A saddletree, the skeleton of a saddle.

No Guts, No Glory

A saddletree has four basic parts:

- The bars

- The fork

- The cantle

- The horn

All of these parts may be modified according to the job or type of riding the saddle is being designed to accommodate, and the fork and bars are also modified to accommodate the difference in horse's backs.

The bars of the saddle determine its fit, in width, length, and angle. The most common types of tree widths are:

- Regular (narrow)

- Semi-quarter horse (medium)

- Quarter horse (wide)

- Arabian (extra wide)

A horse with high withers would most likely require a regular tree, while a wide-backed horse would most likely be best fitted with either a quarter horse or an Arabian tree width. Remember, however, that there is no proven success formula in this area; only seeing and trying is believing.

Design features that can influence rider comfort include the following:

- **Seat length:** 15 inches is considered a normal seat size, especially for women and average men; 16 inches is considered a man's seat size; and 14 inches is usually considered either a youth seat size (see the figure on the following page) or a small woman's seat size. The length is measured from the back of the fork at the base of the horn to the center and top of the cantle.

A child-size western saddle.

- **Slope and padding:** The slope of the seat and the padding can affect the actual amount of sitting area afforded by the seat area.

- **Cantle shape:** The width and height of the cantle.

Another important factor in rider comfort is where on the tree the stirrups are hung. Short-legged riders and small people need their stirrups hung farther toward the rear, while tall, long-legged riders or people with especially long thigh bones need the stirrup hung a little more toward the front in order to be comfortable when riding.

Safety and Comfort before Fashion

When in doubt, always go with a slightly larger seat size. A seat that's too small for you will restrict your freedom of movement, causing you to feel cramped and possibly reduce your security.

Saddle Types

There are a great variety of western saddle types. While all may appear to be similar to the uneducated eye, their various features make them distinctly different. For instance, a roping saddle can easily weigh forty pounds, while today's barrel racing saddle will weigh around twenty pounds. Saddle makers and competitive riders who use each saddle understand the design differences, but the novice or amateur rider can also benefit from knowing these facts, because lifting a heavy roping saddle up on the back of a tall horse may require more upper-body strength than some women and/or children may possess.

The Roping Saddle

Roping is defined as the act of catching an animal—usually a cow, calf, or steer—with a long rope and restraining it by securing one end of the rope to the saddle horn. The horn on a roping saddle must be attached to the saddletree and constructed in a way that will allow both the horn and the saddle to withstand the force of stopping, turning, or dragging a 1,000-pound steer. Simply putting extra wrapping on the horn of a pleasure saddle won't be adequate. If you're a calf roper, you'll also want a low cantle to facilitate your right leg clearing the back of the saddle in a quick dismount to tie up your calf.

The Barrel Racing Saddle

Barrel racing is a mounted competition in which a horse and rider race at full speed around three upright barrels set a specified, measured distance from one another in a specific sequential pattern. A barrel racing saddle is lightweight, with the fenders hung on the tree in a balanced position under the rider. Barrel racing in an equitation saddle (a saddle used mostly for the show ring) would put you and your horse at a disadvantage because the design of an equitation show saddle wouldn't help you when you attempted to position yourself to your horse's best advantage in the tight turns demanded in barrel racing.

The Cutting Saddle

A cutting saddle features an even flatter, more balanced seat design, with the fenders hung directly under the rider's center of gravity and oxbow stirrups. A cutting horse rider must be able to sit centered and

Someone should tell her she's a little overdressed in that parade rig.

balanced in order to be able to move freely and fluidly with the light-ning-quick, catlike moves performed by competitive cutting horses.

The Trail Saddle

A saddle designed primarily for trail riding often features a combination of a high cantle and moderate swells for security. Custom saddles offer extra padding in the seat for comfort on long rides and the addition of small D rings and/or saddle strings in order to attach equipment that a

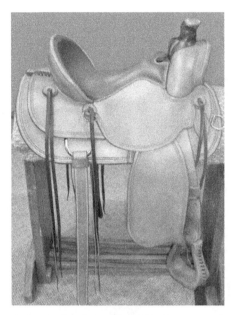

A custom-made trail saddle featuring tie strings, extra D rings, and a high shovel cantle.

This rider's "working" saddle sports a wrapped horn, a bucking roll, and a fencing tool attached to the rear cinch and roper stirrups.

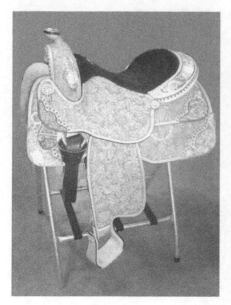

A show saddle (left) and a close-up of its full tooling and silver adornment (right).

trail rider might want to pack along on a day's ride. The stirrups are often hung more toward the front of the tree, promoting a *chair seat,* which is considered more comfortable for the rider when spending long hours in the saddle.

The Show Saddle

A show saddle is used in horse shows and is marked by color (the current fashion trend is toward a very light-colored leather), heavy tooling, and lots of silver. The seat usually displays a fair to extreme degree of slope, designed to secure a rider against the cantle.

The Reining Saddle

Reining is a refined display of movements by horse and rider that's performed through a specified pattern in which the horse and rider control and "work" cattle. A reining saddle must allow for the athletic movement demanded of the horse by the reining patterns, so today's reining saddles use flexible trees and skirt and rigging designs that allow for a "close-contact" type of feel of the horse.

A well-designed all-purpose western saddle displays a slight slope to the seat and a small amount of tooling and silver. This type of saddle could easily be used for both every-day riding, including trail riding, and in shows at the local and regional level.

A design feature of this all-purpose western saddle is the custom-cut skirt, which allows the rider a greater feel of the horse.

Finding a Saddle

Saddles are obtainable today in a number of ways. Used saddles are often advertised in magazines and on the Internet. New, mass-produced saddles are also available through the Internet, as well as in tack stores and from catalogs. Top-of-the-line custom-made saddles are, as you would expect, usually available only through an individual saddle company or maker. When buying a saddle, it is important to make sure you have the right to return the saddle if it doesn't fit your horse correctly.

Don't assume a tack store will have someone on staff who is knowledgeable enough to fit a saddle to you personally. While store personnel may be able to advise you on the features of a particular brand of saddle the store carries, it takes someone whose knowledge of riding and performance extends well beyond what they can read in a brochure to ensure that the saddle you buy is the best one for you and your horse.

Fitting a Saddle

It always amazes me how many riders who are quite knowledgeable in other areas lack the knowledge they need in order to ensure the best fit when buying a saddle. There is no simple solution to choosing a correctly fitting saddle. Time, education, patience, persistence, professional help, and lots of trial runs are the way in which most riders finally make it to success in this important aspect of western riding and performance.

One new innovation that can help reduce some of the grief and frustration inherent in the saddle fit process is the *EQImeasure*. This is a flat piece of space-age material that you heat in your oven and transport to your barn in a pizza-type hot box. Then, while it is still warm and soft, you apply the warmed sheet to the area of your horse's back where the saddle will sit. Using light pressure, you press it to fit your horse's shape. As the mold cools, it will harden. Taking this mold to tack stores or expos when you're shopping for a new saddle can whittle down the potential number of saddle possibilities into a manageable number (perhaps three or fewer), which you may then arrange to bring home in order to try directly on your horse. The EQImeasure can be ordered from Synergist Saddle Company at www.synergistsaddles.com.

To find out more about the important topic of saddles and saddle making before you write a big check for that custom saddle, or when you're desperate because your horse is behaving badly or is lame due to a poorly fitted saddle, I recommend reading *The Western Saddle: A Guide to Selecting and Care of the Western Saddle,* by Carson Thomas.

No matter what type of saddle you're currently using or what you might buy in the future, if the saddle doesn't fit both you and your horse, neither horse nor rider can perform their best.

I once heard someone say that saddle fitting wasn't rocket science, which may be true, but there *is* a lot to it, much more than most owners and riders are made aware of in the normal process of acquiring and riding their horses. During many years of conducting riding and training clinics around the country, I have seen more poorly fitted saddles than ones that fit correctly; the ratio is about 3:1 of poorly fitted to correctly fitted. Poorly fitted saddles can lead to a myriad of performance problems, including bucking, rearing, balking, shortened stride, rough gait, tripping or stumbling, stiffness and resistance to bending, refusal to canter and/or take a particular lead, lameness, and hoof-size variation.

Keep in mind that the saddletree, the frame on which the saddle is built, is the most important part of your saddle. If the saddletree is properly sized to your horse, chances are your saddle will fit well. See the figure on this page for examples of two different sizes of saddletrees.

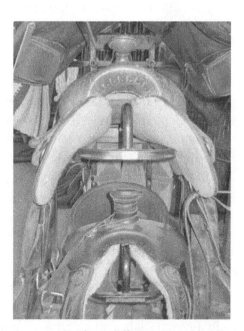

An example of two different sizes of saddletrees. The top saddle shows a medium (semiquarter horse) width tree; the bottom saddle shows a narrow-width tree.

The Horse's Back

In order to explore the topic of saddle fit, we need to start by understanding a little more about the horse's back, the place where the saddle is designed to sit. It may surprise some readers that, from an engineering standpoint, horses weren't designed to carry riders. If you look at a picture of a horse's skeleton, you will notice the spine hangs like a suspended bridge between the front legs and the hind legs, and supports the weight of both the rib cage and the internal organs. A western performance horse carries the heaviest class of saddle used in pleasure and performance riding. When you add the weight of the saddle and the rider together (for instance, a roper weighing 225 pounds riding a saddle weighing 40 pounds), in many cases the horse's weight-carrying capacity is pushed to the limit.

Horses have long, strong muscles down each side of the back called the *longissimus dorsi,* and strong ligaments that support them, but the natural reaction of any horse is to tense these muscles, contracting them when he experiences weight on his back. As a result of this natural reaction, the horse's back actually *hollows,* sinking downward to some degree under a saddle and rider. This piece of information is the "elephant in the living room," because, although it is a critical element affecting saddle fit (when the back changes shape, the "fit" of the saddle is also altered), it is very seldom talked about.

In order to move lightly, without tripping or stumbling, and to access the full athletic potential of his skeleton, a horse must learn how to actively lift his back under a saddle, carrying or supporting the weight of his rider with active abdominal muscles. Because this isn't a horse's natural response, it must become the rider or trainer's responsibility to encourage and educate the horse (especially during early training and conditioning) to carry himself with the efficient muscle groups available, including the abdominal muscles. The rider must first understand this concept, then cause it to happen by using correct aids while riding. How does this involve saddle fit? When the rider causes the horse to move in a good postural alignment, the horse's back will *come up* or lift under the rider, strengthening the muscles of the horse's back and increasing the area of back muscles that make contact with the saddletree.

Riding of this type is called *educated* riding rather than *passenger* riding. It is analogous to a coach's job with an athlete. When an athlete is influenced to practice certain exercises, the muscles necessary to prevent injury and excel in a particular athletic event are strengthened and the athlete's overall performance is improved.

The cause-and-effect principal at work here is even more critical to the horse's well-being and is enhanced or blocked by this same ability to use the back muscles correctly. The horse must be able to swing his back in order to access his natural shock-dissipating system provided by nature to accomplish its job. Scientific study has shown that the oscillations that occur naturally in the horse's back (barrel) are an important part of the way a horse's body dissipates some of the shock waves that occur as the horse's foot strikes the ground. These shock waves travel up the column of the leg into the horse's body. Some of the shock is absorbed in the joints, but in just this past century, science has rediscovered what expert horsemen have know for ages: that the *swing* of the horse's back is what completes the process of dissipating shock from the horse's body, insuring his long-term soundness and serviceability. If the horse is not comfortable in his back, whether from a saddle fit issue or a rider issue, he will tense the area, reducing that swing, and accordingly reduce his ability to defend his body from the debilitating effects of the shock that occur when his hooves strike the ground.

Conformation

Are there additional factors that weigh in on how far we stretch the support system of the horse by riding him? Yes. Conformation—that is, how the horse's physical structure is put together by nature—plays a part in the soundness equation. If your shoe (saddle) rubs or binds you, and you must walk or work in it for any length of time, you will quickly, but often subconsciously, alter your movement pattern in an attempt to find comfort. Left to continue long enough, this adjusted or altered pattern of

---

Not Just an Issue of Comfort

A horse whose back doesn't swing is much more difficult to sit. More importantly, though, a horse who keeps his back muscles tense when saddled will experience a restricted range of motion. He will also suffer from degenerative, career-impeding issues far earlier than will the horse who is enabled—through correct training and saddle fit—to carry a rider on his back with muscles that are flexible and elastic.

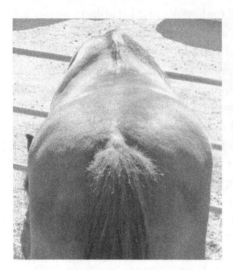

A broad, well-muscled draft horse back.   *A National Show horse with a long, narrow back.*

movement will influence the development of your muscles, causing some to become overdeveloped while others become underdeveloped and weak.

As this situation progresses—especially if you're using your horse in events that require him to access his athletic potential—not only will your horse be pushed closer and closer to the limits of his systems until something breaks, but the cycle of uneven muscle development in the horse's shoulders, hips, and so on will make it even more difficult for any type of a saddle to be correctly fit to your horse's back. Once the cycle has begun, no matter its original triggering factor(s), it can quickly get out of hand, subtracting many years from a horse's useful lifetime and putting a lot of your money in the pocket of your vet.

In the equation of soundness and performance, in only a small percentage of cases does conformation weigh more heavily than training and/or saddle fit and rider balance. Horses whose backs are short and broad are better able to sustain weight with less potential damage to their bodies over years of work (see the figure on this page). The wide, strong back of the draft horse is much less likely to succumb to the stresses of carrying the weight of a 100-pound rider than are the long, narrow back muscles of a thoroughbred (also shown on this page), which can be easily and painfully spasmed by carrying a 200-pound rider in a poorly fitted saddle.

A horse with pronounced, crooked bony alignment in his legs is also a definite candidate for early lameness when ridden, especially if he is used hard, as is a horse who exhibits the conformational balance trait known as being *hip high.*

To thoroughly understand why it is easier to move your limbs when your back is rounded, or up, you have to study the muscles of the body and how they interact with and move or inhibit movement in, the bones and joints. You can explore how a raised versus a hollow back can influence range of motion (movement), balance, and comfort in your horse by doing the following exercise.

1. On your hands and knees, position yourself like a horse who is standing squarely on four legs.

2. Lift your head up and back in the way a horse might who is traveling with his head in the air.

3. Hollow your back by allowing your belly to drop downward toward the ground.

4. Keeping this posture, take a few steps forward, as though you were a horse walking.

5. Now reposition yourself, letting the back of your neck relax and lengthen (as would a horse who has dropped his head and is carrying his neck out of his withers in a relaxed manner). Use your abdominal muscles to lift your back *upward* toward the sky, and walk forward again.

Do you notice how much easier it is to swing your limbs and walk when your back is up? Doing this simple exercise helps you understand what a horse feels like when his back is tied up with tension, whether that tension is being produced by a poorly fitted saddle, a badly balanced rider, or simply by an overabundance of adrenaline in his system, causing the horse to throw his head up in alarm or excitement.

Here's another exercise: While on your hands and knees, have a friend poke you with a blunt, pointed object just between your shoulder blades. What is your reaction? Did you hollow your back? Of course you did. If you then had to move with your back tight, you were again experiencing more effort to cover the ground with your limbs, to say nothing

A correctly adjusted standard breast collar holds the saddle in place without putting pressure on the base of the horse's windpipe.

of any emotional stress you might also have experienced because of the discomfort of this makeshift saddle, which was putting uncomfortable pressure points on your back as you moved. You can now appreciate more fully the importance of saddle fit.

To recap: When back muscles (yours or your horse's) are tight, limbs (yours or your horse's) don't move as freely or as easily as when the back muscles are relaxed and somewhat stretched. Preserving a horse's soundness, sanity, and performance ability depends on correctly fitting the saddle, as well as on adjusting auxiliary equipment such as breast collars (see photos on the next page), rear cinches, and so on to ensure that both saddle and pads stay correctly and comfortably in place as you ride.

In order to fit well, a saddle and saddletree need to:

- Conform to the arc of the horse's back from withers to croup (see photo illustrations of various horse's top lines on the next two pages)

- Match the angle of the horse's shoulder and rib cage

- Allow clearance over the entire length of the spine

- Be designed and fit in a way that distributes the rider's weight evenly over the entire tree without bridging

- Allow room for the horse's shoulder to move freely

- Have a tree suitable in length to the length of the horse's back so the rear edge of the saddle doesn't bump or rub the horse's hip

- Have a seat that allows the rider to sit in balance with gravity

- Be rigged to allow the cinch to "settle" in a place that allows free movement of the horse's elbow without causing cinch sores

Top line shape, back width (wide, medium, narrow), and length (long, medium, short) and withers shape (mutton, medium, high) are all factors that will influence saddle fit. By studying the following photos, you can begin to appreciate the great variety of back shapes in horses.

Yearling filly with nice straight top line.

Haflinger pony with strong weight carry-ing back, fairly level top line.

Mustang mare with well-coupled, strong, level top line.

Quarter horse with good top line.

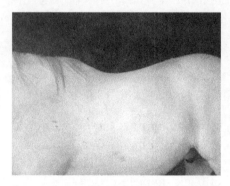

Quarter horse with moderate drop in back.

Short back with a fairly severe drop in top line.

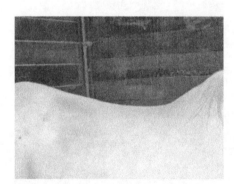

Arabian with severe drop in top line.

Old quarter horse whose top line has more ups and downs than a Disneyland ride.

Rider Balance and Position

Before we leave the topic of saddle fit, the important factors of rider balance and position in the saddle relative to the overall picture of saddle fit needs to be revisited. Western saddles—which are generally built on larger trees and thus have a greater area of contact with the horse's back and therefore the ability to disperse the rider's weight over a broader area of muscle—will, to some extent, buffer the negative consequences of an unbalanced or crooked rider. By contrast, with an English saddle—the lightweight, smaller saddle used in such English riding disciplines such as jumping and dressage—it is possible for an unbalanced rider to quickly create back soreness in a horse. And as noted above, once back soreness has begun, the horse's body will attempt to "adjust" its movement pattern, and you will be off and running on the vicious cycle of poorly fitting equipment, unequal muscular development, and the disruption to training, performance, and soundness that inevitably results.

All saddles (new as well as used) should be examined by turning the saddle upside down and sighting along the length of the tree in order to insure the tree has not become warped. It is always a good idea to compress the saddletree on used saddles with pressure on both sides and from front to back (there should not be any "give" to the tree), to ensure the tree is not cracked or broken.

When trying a new or used saddle on your horse for the first time, be sure that the saddle does not come in contact with your horse's withers, especially when you are mounted. A saddle, well padded or not, that puts pressure on the withers of the horse will eventually cause injury there. Once you're in the saddle, you should also be able to run your fingers under the front edge of your saddle skirt and the saddletree up to

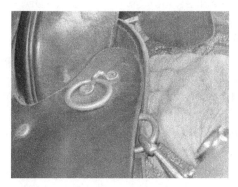

Check the pressure by sliding your hand under the front edge of the saddle. The saddle should not pinch your hand.

your second knuckle without feeling like they are being pinched against the horse's shoulder.

When you're mounted, you should still be able to insert your fingers under the front edge of your saddle and slide them down the entire length of the saddle's front edge without running into so much pressure that your fingers get "stuck."

A thin pad should be used when you are testing saddle fit. If a saddle fits well, a simple blanket to absorb sweat is all you should need. Whether through well-intentioned misdirection or economic strategy, manufacturers have filled the market over the last ten to twelve years with an enormous variety of thick, protective saddle pads. Although these pads serve the consumer (you) by meeting the need to achieve some temporary relief of saddle fit problems, the advertising claims that they protect the horse's back in all circumstances are misleading. No one wants to hear that the saddle doesn't fit the horse, especially after just shelling out up to $3,500 for a fancy new custom-made saddle and perhaps waiting for three or four months for it to be delivered. When the realization finally arrives that the high cost of the saddle didn't guarantee a good fit, riders look for a quick-and-easy solution, and who can blame them? Nine times out of ten, that solution will be a pad of some type, usually one whose advertising claims that it will solve any and all saddle fit issues. The odds of this being true are about the same as winning the lottery. What a pad will do is disguise saddle fit issues. By temporarily making fit issues less obvious, they also delay the process of change (of equipment) long enough to allow either behavior problems or soundness problems to develop in the horse.

Before making your final decision, test-ride a saddle long enough to sweat your horse's back. When you pull the saddle off after your trial ride, your horse's back should be evenly wet. Dry spots on the back under the saddle indicate an inadequate fit. Again, it is best to do this test ride with a thin blanket, not some thick pad. If the saddle *does* fit your horse, adding a thick pad can disturb that fit, making it appear that the saddle is at fault.

Close examination of your horse's back on a regular basis is a must. Training and performance days turn into weeks and months and the muscles of your horse's back will change shape. This is especially true of the young horse who develops more muscle mass as he matures, the horse in poor condition who increases his weight and muscle mass, the obese horse who loses weight and girth size, as his physical condition improves through exercise, and the older horse who gradually loses muscle mass with age.

It is also easy for a slip on muddy footing or a playful buck in a moment of freedom to cause a spinal misalignment or a slightly pulled muscle. A good rider can often feel such a slight change in the way the horse is moving, but in the heat of a competitive season, it may be possible for you to miss subtle signs, especially if the injury or misalignment doesn't result in immediate lameness. If you miss what may, at first, be only a subtle gait change, but you diligently examine your horse's back regularly, you will notice changes in your horse's muscling, which occur when the horse stops using his body or leg(s) in an equally balanced manner. Once you notice such a change, you can set to work solving the mystery of why it has occurred, heading off a potential decrease in performance ability or a soundness issue.

Headgear

A wide variety of headgear is available for the western horse. The right choice usually lies in a combination of factors, including discipline style, fashion, and function. However, just as in choosing a saddle, the more you know about the equipment you use, the greater your chances of selecting the best piece of equipment for the job.

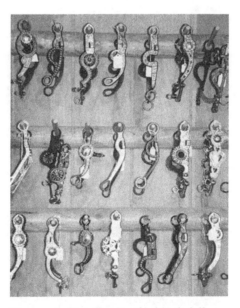

There are literally hundreds of different styles of bits with nearly as many different mouthpieces.

Bits

The topic of bits—their construction, functions, and different styles—at first appears fairly simply and straightforward, just like saddles. But the more you know, the more you find out there is to know, especially if you want to make the best choice of bit for your horse. (See the variety of bit styles in the figures on the preceding page.)

As with saddle fit, finding the right bit is a topic that's like an elephant in the living room. That is to say, there is an aspect of bitting that's seldom considered by the average rider or talked about in books: the condition of your horse's mouth. This includes his dental alignment and the influence that aspect of the horse's physicality has on his ability to give (to the bit), either laterally by rotating his skull (rather than twisting the neck) or longitudinally by flexing at the pole correctly (rather than by breaking at the fourth vertebrae of the neck).

A horse who has an unbalanced mouth:

- Is subject to tension in the muscles of the jaw and skull that creates pain

- May experience condition and/or weight loss issues

- Is more susceptible to bouts of colic

- May become violent if pressure is applied around his pole

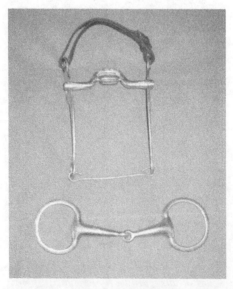

A curb bit with leather chin strap (top) and an egg butt snaffle bit (bottom).

Horses need regular (once a year at least) dental maintenance from a skilled dentist. Floating by with a veterinarian who has not had extended education in today's modern dental practices will not address the numerous issues that can arise in a horse's mouth and that an equine dentist is equipped and educated to correct. It is not uncommon for riders, trainers, and owners to misdiagnose behavior issues stemming from a horse's need for dental work. The first potential cure is often a change of bits, but any improvement this particular cure offers seldom lasts, because it usually only addresses the superficial symptoms, rather than the underlying cause.

Most young horses today are started either in a snaffle or a hackamore. When their basic education is well established, including correctly responding by moving smoothly away from a light pressure cue of the rein touching the side of the neck, they are graduated to a curb bit.

Common mouthpieces found in curb bits are the Mullen, the Mona Lisa, the Salinas, the spade, and the "broken mouth." Different associations, like the National Reining Horse Association, the Quarter Horse Association, and the United States Equestrian Federation have various requirements about bit types. These requirements can specify length of shank, the structure of the mouthpiece (including thickness), where the rein is attached, and chin strap construction. Since these requirements can vary from one organization to another, from class to class, and also with the age of a horse (under USEF rules, for instance, a junior horse who is 5 years old or younger may be shown in any class in either a hackamore or snaffle bit), the more you learn about bits, the better.

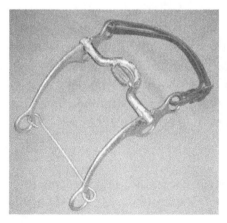

A curb bit with a moderate port and a roller.

The curb strap or chain should allow for two fingers to be inserted between it and the horse's jaw.

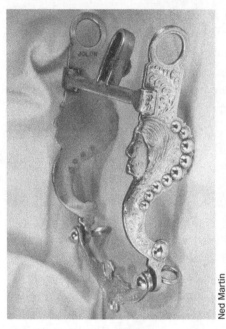

Ned Martin

Ned Martin

Bit making is truly an American art form, and many of the old western bits, especially the style known as the "spade bit," are now highly prized, extremely collectible, and very valuable.

In addition to regulating which bits may be used in different types of classes, organizations also specify what types of reins may be used and how the rider must hold the reins when riding with a particular bit. If you compete with your horse, one of your jobs is to know the rules of the association that governs your discipline and to keep up with any yearly rule changes. In nearly all organizations, competitors may be penalized or even eliminated for incomplete or incorrect appointments.

A great source of information on the history of western bits and their makers is *Bit and Spur Makers in the Vaquero Tradition,* a book by Ned and Jody Martin that is loaded with clear photos showing designs, signatures (of the maker), mouthpiece styles, and more, and documenting the work of over a hundred bit makers from rare to well known.

Headstalls

Headstalls come in nearly as many styles as saddles and it seems each discipline has it preferred "type." The following photos show only a portion of the variety of different styles.

The Absolute Basics Everyone Needs to Know About Bits

There are two primary types: snaffles and curbs. The difference between the two types is not decided by the mouthpiece, but rather is determined by where the reins connect to the bit and where the bit applies pressure on the horse's head and mouth. Catalog descriptions and bit designing trainers aside, a bit is only a *snaffle* if the pressure from the rein is delivered directly to the horse's mouth, rather than intensified by a level action of any type.

- A snaffle bit gives better lateral control than a curb.

- A curb offers more flexing and stopping influence than a simple snaffle.

- The bit alone cannot stop a horse if he doesn't want to stop.

- Horses have different-shaped mouths, and this may influence which bits they prefer or which bits will work best.

- A bit that's too narrow can pinch a horse.

- The severity of a bit can be altered by how high or low it sits in the horse's mouth.

- The greater the ratio of the shank length below the mouthpiece to the length above the mouthpiece (the part where the headstall is attached), the more severe the bit action, regardless of the type of mouthpiece.

- A curb (chin) strap or chain must be in place in order for a curb bit to function as a curb and the tightness of the chin strap/chain impacts the severity of the bit, as does the height of an arched mouthpiece.

The only really new innovations in bit design in the past hundred years are those recently introduced by the Myler Bit Company. Those bits feature uniquely jointed mouthpieces.

A working headstall with brow band and throatlatch, shown with a snaffle bit, slobber straps, and rope reins

A split ear headstall, decorated with silver conchos, shown with a loose ring, twisted wire snaffle, and a dropped noseband cavason (gymkhana competitor).

A shaped ear headstall with generous amounts of sterling silver with gold overlay, shown with a curb bit (western pleasure competitor).

A very narrow, shaped-ear show headstall with silver decoration, designed to compliment the refined head of an Arabian, shown with a Santa Barbara spade bit, romal reins, and a rawhide pencil bosal.

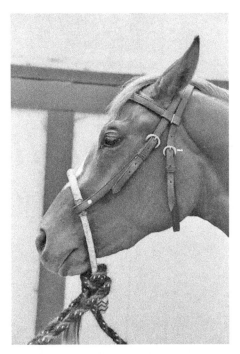

A hackamore with a working headstall attached to a rawhide bosal, with horsehair reins.

Chapter 3

Training Your Horse Successfully

Getting Started

One of the great sages of the twentieth century, George Carlin, wrote a piece entitled "Ninety-Nine Things You Need to Know" (from his book *When Will Jesus Bring the Pork Chops*). For the purpose of expediency, I have excerpted from his list the ones that particularly apply to horse training. Anyone who is already a horse trainer will recognize the truth in this list. If you have yet to become a horse trainer, retain this list, because the longer you work with horses, the more sense it will make and the funnier it will become (and at some future date, you'll need to laugh).

- Some of the things you need to know are things you already know.

- Some of the things you need to know are things you only think you know.

- Some of the things you need to know are things you used to know and then forgot.

- Some of the things you need to know are things you don't yet know you need to know.

- Some of the things you need to know are things known only by people you don't know.

- Some of the things you need to know are things nobody knows.

Reading up on Training

Let me give you one further piece of advice. You can't learn how to train a horse from a book. Only the horse and possibly another human can teach you how to communicate with, and thus gain the cooperation of, a horse. A book can be a good place to start your journey of learning, however, especially if it is a good book on training (as you will discover, there are many books on the topic and not all of them give complete or accurate information). A good book is one that gives you:

- A greater understanding of the journey you are on (or about to undertake), by giving you an overview of that journey, a context in which to place the various content that you will need to accumulate and acquaint yourself with on your road trip of learning

- Definitions of the various learning levels and thoughts about how and when to advance your horse through each one

- Ideas and tools for answering the questions and solving the problems that may arise for you and your horse, in each level

So start your journey with a book. Better yet, start with several. I recommend the following:

- The "Charlie" series by Suzanne Norton Jones (*Charlie, Please and Thank You; Charlie, Comes a Horseman: Bill;* and *Charlie, A Little Knowledge*). When you consider yourself ready for high school study, try her *Whisper I, II,* and *III* series.

- *Horse Gaits, Balance and Movement* by Susan Harris should be in the reference library of every trainer, whether amateur or professional.

- You will have to hunt for *The Schooling of the Western Horse* by John Richard Young, because it has long been out of print. Nonetheless, it is a western classic that you may be able to find on the Internet or through used book dealers. The information in its pages makes it well worth the hunt.

- I also recommend the books of Mark Rashid as well as *Building Your Dream Horse* by Charles Wilhelm.

Getting Together with Horse Advisers

After you've finished reading your first (or first dozen) book(s), your next step should be to get more three-dimensional input by listening to and observing an adviser. Some of today's well-known advisers, or *horse behaviorists,* as I like to call them, are Clinton Anderson, Buck Brannaman, Harry Whitney, Linda Tellington-Jones, Chris Cox, Charles Wilhelm, Cleve Wells, John and Josh Lyons, Richard Shrake, Pat Parelli, Monte Roberts, and Lynn Palm.

These advisers can be accessed in "short-course" form on specific topics at major equestrian expositions like Equine Affaire, in local clinics, through their instructional DVDs and videos, and on the RFD TV channel. If you have to travel with your horse in order to access these experts, consider it time and money well spent. A good education costs money, but it's generally cheaper than a hospital bill and will help ensure an enjoyable relationship with your horse.

Although perhaps not the ideal one-on-one learning environment of a private lesson, the above type of learning opportunities will provide further clarification on the training systems and techniques with which you've already begun to acquaint yourself through your reading. Remember, first you need to understand the concept (system), then you need to learn how to use the tools (techniques) correctly and safely. You'll also need a teacher or a coach somewhere along the line to help clarify your understanding by supervising your execution. You can participate in some clinics with no prior experience, but if you do, realize that you will be like a kid in kindergarten. The clinician's job will be to keep you safe, clarify the process, and prepare you for what you will encounter in the next step in your learning curve. If you study some of your topics beforehand by reading about them, you will be able to move through the material faster and get more out of your course/clinic tuition. This is a repeating cycle in the process of learning about horses, whether you are focusing on learning to train them or to ride well.

Finding a Coach

To flesh out, polish, and finish your education process in training a horse, you can engage in direct work with a mentor, a trainer, or a training coach on a daily (or at least weekly) basis. While this type of education will certainly offer you the greatest chance to learn the lessons needed to successfully train—or maintain the training of—your horse, the unfortunate reality is that good, well-qualified professionals simply aren't readily available in all parts of the country. Quality trainers and coaches don't grow on trees, and in the case of horses, poor or erroneous information is definitely not better than none at all. If you've had no education at all, at least you may know that you don't know. If you've had erroneous input, you are most likely operating under false assumptions, ones that could easily get you hurt and/or ruin your horse, or at the very least slow or stagnate your progress toward your goals.

Getting Comfortable with a System

There are many "systems" of training horses, especially if you include all types of riding in all nations around the globe. While we can argue the benefits of any given system, if the horse is enabled to safely work (or play) with humans after the "training," the person applying the method can claim success. Most systems are built around a specific type of job or discipline and so are structured in a way that works on preparing the horse for that job. That being the case, you will find that each system will vary somewhat and will emphasize slightly different aspects of the horse's performance and build his fitness and athleticism to that end. Learning which system works best for you and your horse will be a part of the journey you undertake when you decide to train a horse or to have one trained, but it will be helpful if you keep in mind the job(s) around which the system(s) was designed.

Be prepared to make mistakes. If you don't, you'll be the first trainer in history who hasn't made them. The hesitation and paralysis that can come from a fear of making mistakes with your horse can easily be worse than a wrong move or a small error in judgment on your part. Horses require and respect clarity and consistency from their leader(s). Your horse will have a hard time accepting you as his leader if you constantly project a lack of faith in yourself and your decisions.

While it's hard to know in advance without experience which system may be best for you and your horse, knowing that more than one system exists gives you the power of choice. With time and effort you can investigate and compare different systems, gradually making the various "tools" or techniques your own. Waiting until you are having a serious problem with a horse isn't the best way to approach learning how to train horses. Under such circumstances you will feel a great deal of pressure, and pressure is a major ingredient in getting both people and horses hurt. If you find yourself in such a situation, it may be best to hire a professional trainer to help you and your horse through the tough or dangerous problem, getting you both headed in the right direction. You will have learned by observing the more experienced professional, and hopefully you will be able to continue on with the training of your horse afterward. The training, care, and handling of horses is a lifelong learning course, so being in a hurry doesn't offer much of a reward and can end up costing a lot in missed opportunities and downtime for horse and/or rider.

The Universal Principles

No matter which system of training you elect to follow, the three Ps—patience, persistence, and practice—will carry the same weight. When you read books on training or attend educational clinics, you hear professionals talk about these concepts all the time. So if these keys to success are no secret, why aren't more people successful at training their own horse? The answer to that question can be condensed into three more words: interpretation, execution, and follow-through.

Interpretation

In order to produce or to follow an instruction, you've got to clearly understand that instruction. When you hear a comparison-based word—like the word "big," for instance—you will draw a conclusion about what that word means, and how it fits into the picture of instruction based on your own experience of the word. For example, if someone who is trying to describe the size of something, says it's "big as a house" and is thinking about a sixty-five-room mansion, and the only house you've ever experienced is a one-bedroom home, there is likely to be some discrepancy between what you heard and what you understood. The speaker is using descriptive language to help convey an idea to you or to give you instructions in order to enable you to execute a particular training technique with your horse. Any discrepancy in interpretation of the instructions on your part will leave you heading in a faulty direction. When that happens, the results you are after may not happen and you will be stuck wondering what went wrong, or may even leave you thinking that the technique(s) were faulty or don't work for you or your horse. The person feeding you the information can influence your conclusions, which can be further clarified if you allow that person to observe that your execution indicates that although you might have heard the messages, you didn't clearly understand them or what they meant. If you proceeded without further input to build something based on your inaccurate understanding, you might indeed succeed in changing your horse in some way, but the likelihood that the outcome would resemble what the speaker had intended would be remote.

Remember: Keeping that in mind, take a look at the first (and perhaps most important) key to success in training, patience. The horse's sense of "enough" time and a human's sense of "enough" time is seldom synchronized; humans have the tendency to have a (much) shorter version of what constitutes "enough." It can take many years of working with and around horses to reset your clock to horse time and learn to correctly read their body language. So when you hear or read the word "patience" in relationship to training a horse, as a human you are likely to be thinking three seconds, three minutes, or three hours, while your horse-savvy trainer and the horse are likely to be imagining three days, three weeks, or three months (if not longer). Next time you get stuck in your training, try employing the patience strategy and simply observe who becomes impatient first—you or the horse. If you truly learn this lesson, you will be well on your way to becoming a successful horse communicator, which is a huge step in the journey to becoming a successful horse trainer.

Execution

How you give a cue or an aid, when you do it, what your emotional state is as you do it, how well you read the horse's response and respond to the horse's response to you—all these aspects separate the amateur from the successful professional. Both may have an extensive knowledge of the elements of a particular technique, but only the one who has the ability to execute cues or aids in a correct and timely manner will succeed in getting cooperation from the horse, educating the horse, and making him a better athlete and partner in the process.

Remember: Here is where the second key to success, persistence, becomes important. Persistence is a close twin of patience but not an identical one. Patience can lead you to sit with your horse facing a stream he does not want to cross until the cows come home.

Persistence means you will not only wait patiently for your horse to accept the fact that he will put his feet in water before dawn, but it also means you will continue to put the question to him. Using whatever techniques and knowledge (of his nature) you possess, you will, without hurrying him, keep his mind engaged on your conversation and the task at hand. Patience is passive persistence. Persistence is active patience.

The most common problem people tend to encounter when trying to fit the key of persistence in the door of training is the arrival of that unwanted visitor called aggressive behavior. A horse who is pressured can exhibit aggressive behavior, but mostly it will be the human member of the team

Horse trainer job requirement number one: infinite patience!

who experiences a tendency to escalate the use of force when applying a particular technique or when the first key, patience, has been lost.

Follow-through

The training of a behavior (in the horse) has several stages.

- Stage 1: The first stage is getting the horse to understand what it is you desire from him.

- Stage 2: The second stage is getting his agreement to perform the behavior.

- Stage 3: The third stage is repeating the same cue(s) or aid(s) enough times to know your horse understands, without the shadow of a doubt, what it is you expect of him. In other words, he will give the same response to a cue most of the time. This is where most amateurs and even some professionals stop.

- Stage 4: I call the fourth stage the *habit stage,* and it is a step beyond the horse simply understanding and performing a response out of choice.

Remember: In the fourth stage, practice moves the horse from a choice to a habitual response. Practice at this level is follow-through. While the distinction between choice and habit may seem to be a minor one, especially if the horse offers a correct response most of the time, it can become a critical one in times of stress. A horse who will stand still, stop, bend, go, back up, and so on only when he is in his comfort zone is not "well trained." Such a horse is potentially a greater danger to the humans who handle him, than either the untrained horse or the horse who is spoiled.

John Lyons, working with a horse on a saddling issue during a demonstration in Sacramento, California, commented to the audience, "If it takes two people to saddle a horse, you shouldn't be riding that horse!" As he went on to work with the animal, who had a fear of being saddled, he noted, "It's not untrained horses people get hurt on, it's the 'broke' horse." What Mr. Lyons was attempting to convey to his audience with that statement was the importance of follow-through in training and how often the lack of it creates situations in which horses end up injuring their riders or handlers.

Now at first glance it may seem as though follow-through and practice are the same thing, but while they may be considered twins, they aren't identical twins.

- Practice consists of a routine you do with a horse: an act, an aid, a cue or a series of acts, aids, or cues given with a specific performance result (from the horse) in mind. Practice is focused on learning and muscular development.

- Follow-through is practice expanded. Follow-through takes the results of practicing a particular exercise and enlarges the playing field, asking the horse to continue to produce the practiced behavior in new, different, more demanding, emotionally heightened, and explosive situations, until the horse performs the desired behavior without deviation, without delay, and without an attitude of "Let me take a message and get back to you," or "Don't bother me right now, I'm busy having a panic attack," or "Get outta my face—I'm running for my life!"

The Order of the Lessons

The following information is offered as a general road map of a route that has proven tried and true over hundreds and even thousands of years.

Both the order of lesson focus and the order of exercise introduction and practice are of importance if this map is to get you and your horse to your destination in good order and in a reasonable amount of time.

Controlling the Gas Pedal

A horse who does not move forward willingly upon command (whether in hand or mounted) is an accident waiting to happen. Such a horse is more likely to buck, rear, and/or run backward in times of stress and is definitely going to get himself and his rider or handler in trouble at some point. So the go-forward lesson of prompt obedience to the rider's leg, seat, and/or voice aid(s) becomes the first lesson we teach the horse by virtue of its importance in the overall picture of training. The following mounted exercises are ridden to teach and emphasize the go-forward lesson):

- Transitions upward *between* gaits

- Transitions upward *within* the gaits (shown in the following photos)

These exercises must be practiced and refined with the focus divided into two parts.

- Part one is the horse's response time. The horse must learn to respond promptly and fully under all circumstances to the rider's aids or requests to move forward.

- The second focus is *frame*. The horse must learn to carry himself forward in balance.

In these photos you can see a young (4-year-old) paint mare being schooled in transitions upward within a gait (jog to trot). In the left photo, note how little engagement the mare's hind leg is exhibiting under her belly. By contrast, in the right photo, the mare complies with the rider's command for more impulsion and moves into a more powerful trot, bringing her hind leg much further under her body (to the rear cinch).

Improving balance and prolonging soundness in the horse will depend on your ability to call upon your horse to use specific muscle groups when he moves forward over the ground carrying you on his back. The physically round appearance or outline of a horse, which can be observed when a horse is using the correct muscle groups to move over the ground, is also what is referred to directly or indirectly when such words as "frame," "on the bit," "supple," and "engaged" are used in the discussion of training horses. The figure on this page demonstrates an inefficient posture, called the low position, that places too much stress on the horse's front end.

To assist in developing your mental pictures of this term in action, study the drawings and illustrations in the book *Horse Gaits, Balance and Movement* by Susan Harris. To produce a good working frame in a horse, the rider must successfully control the gas pedal and all the "doors" and be able to relax the horse in the jaw, neck, and back. The need for relaxing the neck and jaw of the horse is where the application of the western flexing and bending exercise(s), often referred to as *getting give*, enter the training picture.

While this horse, with her head and neck carried in such a low position, may be stretching her top line, her lack of engagement from behind leaves her rider without the ability to ask the horse to pick up her forehand. This low-headed trend in pleasure horses is gradually being phased out of the show ring, as riders, judges, and officials realize that the posture stresses the horse's front end and does not allow the rider good control of the horse.

Lateral Control

The second focus in training is lateral control. This stage of training addresses directional control of the horse's body through suppling of the jaw, neck, and rib cage, and by isolation and control of the individual body parts (forehand, ribs, hindquarters) of the horse. Mounted exercises to improve lateral control include:

- Suppling the jaw by asking the horse to *give* his jaw to the pressure of the rein (one side at a time), then his poll (where the skull joins the neck), by giving and turning *only* his head, in either direction, created by a swiveling action at the poll, and the neck by relaxing the neck muscles and curving or flexing his neck (in both directions) in order to follow the rein and the rider's leading hand. These individual lessons take time to communicate to the horse and for the horse to understand and become comfortable in executing. The horse must be taught to produce these behaviors, or *gives,* both while standing still and when in motion, which is another reason why this part of his education will take place over a longer period of time. Hurrying the responses in this stage will cause the horse to skip learning to give in some sections of his anatomy. These stuck places can make it easier for the horse to ignore his rider's lateral requests at critical moments and/or will subtract from the beauty and quickness of an athletic performance because fluidity of movement can only come when the horse's energy is allowed to move freely through his body without tension or stiffness.

- Relaxing the back and getting give in the rib cage. This will occur to some degree as a result of getting give in the horse's neck, but it is repeated and accurate riding of what are commonly called the *school figures*: patterns composed of circles, straight lines, and bending lines that supple the horse's joints and back and lead to him engage his hind legs more deeply under his body as he moves.

- Isolation and directional control of the shoulders, hips, and ribs using exercises such as turn-on-the-forehand and turn-on-the-haunches, roll backs, and so on.

Every show, pleasure, and trail rider should master the exercise known as leg yielding. Speed games, reining, and cutting riders and their horses would benefit greatly from mastering the gymnastic power-lifting exercise known in English riding circles as the *shoulder-in and counter shoulder-in.*

A young paint mare demonstrates softness through her entire body on a bending line, in both trot and canter. The photos show a relaxed head and neck and an even bend throughout the spine as the horse willingly follows her rider's leading rein cue into the turn.

Control of the Brakes

The third focus in training is control of the horse's forward drive, or control of the brakes. When driving a car, to gain refined control of your vehicle you've got to learn how to apply the brakes in small amounts at just the right time and not just keep shutting the engine off. In the same way, although the initial training in this stage of learning may deal with disengaging the horse's power source entirely for safety considerations, eventually you've got to learn to apply the brakes in smaller amounts. Mounted exercises for tuning up the brakes include:

- Downward transitions from all gaits

- Use of the verbal "whoa!"

- Small circles around the rider's inside leg to disengage the horse's power train (hind end) if the horse fails to obey lighter cues

In mastering the brakes under all circumstances, the rider needs to sort out and focus on the different levels of accomplishment progressively. If a harsh bit is used as the primary method for stopping or controlling forward energy in a horse, long-term results will have a diminishing rate of return, directly related to the severity of the bit and the lack of education and understanding on the part of the horse.

A horse who is running forward, unbalanced, and/or emotionally out of control makes rider safety the highest priority. But except in isolated instances, if such a state is a regular occurrence, a return to ground work is called for. Fine-tuned control of a horse's biomechanical system cannot be achieved until a rider can gain some control of the horse's mind.

While it may seem that it would only be sensible to give the ability to stop a horse the highest priority in the training steps, brakes are actually the third focus in mounted training, because (as silly as it may sound), you've got to get the horse moving forward on command before you can teach him how to stop on command.

If you're a good horseman who wants to have any hope of putting a balanced, willing stop on your horse, you know that you've got to teach the stop or whoa separately on each side of the horse's body before you ask for it on both sides at the same time. Ergo, the lateral control focus also steps ahead of control of the brakes in mounted work. *Unmounted* training, however, should have begun to instill a verbal braking cue before the horse is ever mounted.

Other aspects make this seemingly illogical order of training appropriate. First, a horse who won't go willingly forward when asked is potentially more dangerous than a horse who is hard to stop. Second, a horse must have time to learn how to slow and/or stop with a rider's weight on his back. Without that learning, you will be forced to stop the horse in one of two ways, both of which can backfire.

- The first is discomfort or pain in his mouth from the bit. This method, while it is used inadvertently by a great many riders, frequently creates what is known as a *hard-mouthed horse*—that is, one who is insensitive to pain and/or the pressure of the bit.

- The second method requires timing and some physical strength; therefore, it is not equally available to all riders. The method involves disengaging the horse's hind legs from under his body (thereby reducing their driving power), by bending his head and neck around one of his shoulders, and forcing his nose to the rider's knee. The limitations in this method of stopping a horse involve the horse's ability to balance himself (it is fairly easy to throw a horse to the ground by unbalancing him laterally at just the wrong moment—movie stuntmen do it all the time) and timing (if a horse is truly bolting, especially with the bit clamped in his teeth, it would take a strong and well-positioned rider to effectively override the horse's control of his tense neck muscles, in

The photo on the left shows a common rider hand position error. Too-long reins have forced the rider to raise her hands as she asks her horse to back. The raised position of her hand has, in turn, raised the horse's head, making it difficult for the horse to engage his hind end and back smoothly. In the photo on the right, the rider has shortened her reins and lowered her hands. The horse has correspondingly lowered his head and is now executing the back-up in a much better frame.

order to bend the animal's neck when he didn't want to give it. The second mounted focus works on lateral suppling for just that reason.

The horse has to be given time, through repeated work, to learn how to understand and correctly respond to pressure from the bit and reins by releasing his jaw, pole, and finally his neck. Doing this training slowly, without pressure, teaching the horse first on one side and then the other also allows the horse's body to prepare itself for the halt or "whoa" by engaging the hind legs, flexing the joints, and bringing his mass to a halt without the pain and stiffness or jarring in his limbs and joints. Mastering the way in which energy is allowed to be expressed "out the front door" in this way is necessary in order to eventually bring the horse into a "frame" and collect him. If you have intimidated your horse with the bit, when it comes time to put him together or compress his body, you won't be able to get to his full potential to compress himself, because he will constantly try to stay behind your hands and the pressure of the bit.

Professional horsemen know how important good hands and a light feel of a horse's mouth are in getting a good performance from the horse. It is difficult for amateurs or novices to accomplish such a feel with consistency, not because they don't understand the concept, but because to do so requires riders be in total control of their own bodies and muscular responses. Anyone who is a good rider will tell you that feel takes focus, balance, and practice to develop. A quiet rider without *feel* may be able to successfully ride a well-schooled, sensitive horse, but he cannot train a horse to perform at that level, and it will be difficult for him to keep such a horse's responses from deteriorating without the assistance of a professional.

Some Training Tools

The three following sections explore three powerful tools of work in a round pen, work over ground poles (cavaletti), and riding on uneven topography (trails).

The Round Pen

The *round pen* has become a very popular training tool in the last fifteen years (see the photo on this page for a round pen). Today it is impossible to go to any large equine expo without seeing at least one trainer demonstrating some training technique or other in a circular arena. The circular arena is not a new gimmick in training horses and indeed can trace its history back at least as far as the eighteenth century in France. What today's clinicians have brought to the attention of the general public (meaning the average horse rider/owner), is the way in which the round pen can be used as a tool in establishing herd hierarchy and adjusting a horse's emotional levels.

Why Is the Shape of the Pen So Important?

A horse can become stuck if he faces directly into a corner with his head. If that happens, the horse's flight instinct is thwarted and the horse can experience a buildup of pressure, which may push him into

An example of an enclosed round pen. A round pen can be constructed of pipe panels or solid panels, should be at least 6 feet high, and can have a diameter of from 50 to 80 feet.

Sending a trained horse around a round pen to the left.

behaviors such as kicking, rearing, striking, or trying to climb out of a restrictive enclosure. In an enclosure with no corners, the horse's free flow of movement is less likely to be interrupted. Encouraging and allowing a horse to move forward is one the secrets of success when establishing physical and mental control over the animal. A horse's first defense is to run or flee. In a round pen situation, a trainer can access the best of both worlds. By the use of body language through positioning and intent, the trainer can allow the horse the freedom to flee, at the same time controlling his forward movement without blocking him completely. This directed movement tends to defuse a horse's potentially explosive energy. When the horse feels threatened and wants to run, his body produces adrenaline, which fuels the flight process. If flight is prevented, the adrenaline is trapped in the horse's body and brain, giving him the heebie-jeebies and making any type of concentration difficult if not impossible.

Once a significant amount of adrenaline has entered the horse's bloodstream (no matter what the initial cause of that release), it is difficult for the horse to focus. Instead he feels a need to exercise his most basic instinct; which is to bolt, run, or move off. As the horse moves, adrenaline abates, especially if the horse is gradually contained and directed into a circle by the round shape of the arena design. If whatever negative consequences the horse was anticipating fail to occur, most horses will begin to reconsider their position on the degree of potential danger, and their body and brain will respond by ceasing to pump adrenaline into the system. The golden rule of training—"make the right thing (whatever you want the horse to do) easy, and the wrong thing (the behavior you do not want the horse to choose) difficult"—can be effected by judiciously and periodically stepping into the horse's flight path with enough energy or commotion to cause him to change his direction. This way, you begin to affect his thinking process, engaging

Using body language and physical positioning, the trainer reverses the horse with an inward turn.

his brain, because the direction of his movement is being controlled and that control is typically exerted by a dominant horse in the herd.

If you control the direction of movement, you become lead horse. If you continue to behave in an understandable (to the horse), nonthreatening manner, you will automatically take on the role of protector, as the horse you are working comes to acknowledge your authority as leader. Horses in a herd will take their flight cue from the lead mare. If a horse is disruptive, behaving like a drama queen, and the lead horse does not sanction the behavior by agreeing to join with the horse who is continually having hysterical panic attacks and bolting, the mare will soon discipline the overanxious worrywart by driving that horse away from the protection of the herd, to its periphery, keeping the disruptive dissident at arm's length, until the horse settles down and comes to his senses.

Heather Hutter

The wayward animal is only allowed to return to a protected place within the herd upon realizing he must look to the lead horse for danger cues, rather than go running off every time a rabbit jumps or a twig snaps, thus sparking the herd into unnecessary, debilitating, and potentially dangerous flight when no threat actually exists in reality.

When a trainer expertly exerts pressure through presence and body language on a horse who is fleeing around the parameter of a round pen, the trainer is establishing his or her role as leader of their herd of two, communicating to the horse that there is no real need for fear and/or hysteria, and indeed that the horse is overreacting to the circumstances. When this is done by knowledgeable riders, the horse who is fleeing frequently has an epiphany during the session and bonds with the leader. In this case, not only will the horse settle down, but frequently—after a period of "thinking about it" and perhaps some additional body positioning work at a much slower pace, by the "lead horse" in the center of the arena (the trainer or human working the horse)—the horse will actually move toward his leader/protector, seeking approval, protection, and reassurance.

Round penning does not mean chasing a horse around in a circle until it is physically and emotionally exhausted. Used in that manner, the tool can do permanent physical (if not psychological) damage.

Learning the Body Language of the Round Pen

It's pretty simple really. Because horses use body language to communicate with one another, they also read our body language. The problems occur when people aren't aware of the body language messages they are sending to the horse. Position is everything in body language: the position of a horse's ears, the positioning (shape) of his nostrils, a movement of his neck, a lifting or turning of his head, a positioning of a hip or foot, and so on. So let's start learning how to speak simple sentences from the perspective of positioning (ourselves relative to the horse) in the round pen. Looking at the horse from the side, divide him down the middle mentally. This *middle line* will fall somewhere just behind the withers and shoulder of the horse, a little to the front of the middle of his barrel. As the horse moves away from you around the pen, either on his own or because you've exerted your leader horse status and pushed or sent him away, you will retire to the center of the round pen, where you will stand

Heather Hulter

The trainer steps in with a heightened level of intent evidenced in her body language in order to encourage greater forward impulsion in the horse she is working.

in a neutral spot, exactly centered in the space the two of you are sharing. When you leave this space, it will be in order to influence the horse. When he responds to your influence and/or when you want to release him from pressure, you will return to the neutral space at the center of the round pen.

If you move toward the horse on a line, which would cause you to meet the horse at a point *in front* of his shoulder, your actions will tend to slow or turn the horse. With a horse who is extremely emotional and moving very fast, you'll want to move well ahead of the shoulder line in order to have the time to exert enough influence to block the horse's forward movement. Remember, a train can stop, but it may take a half mile to be able to do so once the engineer (the horse's brain) has thrown the switch, so lying on the tracks at night dressed in black in front of a speeding train because you believe the engineer won't run over you is a pretty stupid thing to do. A horse can stop or reverse much more quickly than a train, but you may need to use a lot of attention-getting body language the first few times you attempt to reverse a half ton of emotion-driven muscle and bone against its will—think neon yellow slicker, two bright red flags, and a floodlight pointed at you so the engineer sees you in plenty of time to stop before you and the train (horse) are trying to occupy the same space at the same time. Of course, some horses are more sensitive than others and all you have to do is *start* to move toward his nose, and he will turn in the opposite direction. Each horse will be different. Reading his intent accurately and learning how to clearly communicate your own is what learning how to train a horse is all about.

If you move toward the horse from the central neutral point on a line, which would bring you to the horse behind his midline—say, at his hip—his tendency will be to speed up. If he's lazy, you may need more than your voice or a wave of your hand in order to drive him forward and away from you. When you are driving the horse forward, or away from you, remember that your goal is not to frighten the wits out of the poor animal, but only to bring enough pressure to bear in order to cause him to move in the direction you intended for him to travel. The lead horse controls the space. It is a law of horsedom, and it is one you must observe and obey or you will find yourself being moved around by your horse and *he* will then be the leader of your herd of two, no matter what your opinion of your comparative intelligence.

Stepping back away from the horse releases pressure. A release of pressure offers the horse both safety and time to think. As you work the language of your body position in the round pen in relation to the horse,

Clearly defining the leadership role in your relationship with your horse is one of the important goals of round pen work.

you are proving your status to the horse, because you are controlling his direction and will ultimately control his speed as well. Stepping into the horse's space will pressure him; stepping back from the horse offers him an opportunity to turn and investigate you. A horse's natural curiosity is a tool you can use to control his choices, and it is second in intensity only to his sense of caution and self-preservation by flight.

As you refine this dance of positioning between you and the horse, you will eventually be able to turn the horse in both directions and you will be able to turn him away from you or in toward you when you do turn him.

Remember: The preceding basics are far from the end of the learning curve for this particular tool. How to read the body language of horses in order to handle the variety of situations and personalities, which can potentially be addressed using the round pen, is something that takes time and instruction from a professional. What has been discussed is only enough information to give your cabbie directions to your hotel.

Cavalletti

Ground poles are a valuable training tool often overlooked by the western disciplines. When they are mounted on end supports, which allow them to be adjusted in three basic heights, they are known as *cavalletti.*

These adjustable-height poles promote the following in the horse: increased focus, increased range of motion (both extension and flexion), balance, impulsion, and tempo. See the photos on this and the next page for examples of cavalletti.

When a horse is ridden through poles in a relaxed, correct frame, the work promotes increased stretching of the horse's top line, enhancing correct muscle development in the hindquarters, loin, back, shoulder, and neck. That's a lot of pluses for some oversized pickup sticks. In a flat arena, the use of cavalletti in training gives many of the same benefits as riding a horse over terrain. Because it is easier to buy and set up cavalletti in an arena than it is for many riders to find the time for or the access to work on the trail, this particular training tool is well worth investigating.

To truly expand your education with this tool, however, you can't be a western-style snob, since the most authoritative book on the topic, *Cavalletti, Schooling of Horse and Rider over Ground Rails*, by the great German trainer and Olympic gold medallist Reiner Klimke, is an English discipline text. Want to be the best? Learn to think out of the box. Study and use this valuable tool in your training program.

A young horse being introduced to cavalletti, which have been adjusted to their lowest height, is allowed to walk quietly through the poles. Here she demonstrates the desirable stretched-top-line posture, lowering her head and neck as she steps over the poles.

The same mare, confident in her ability to handle the questions raised by the poles, now trots in a relaxed manner through the same line, demonstrating excellent balance and engagement and a correct frame. Note the increased flexion in the joints of the elevated diagonal pair of legs, created by the exercise.

In this photo, the cavalletti have been raised several inches, so the power, balance, and joint flexion challenges have been increased. The mare entered the line without balancing herself, and consequently finds her front legs too heavily weighted to comfortably answer the cavalletti challenge of this line. Instead, she looks as though she is about to "nose-dive" into the poles she is trying to negotiate.

This photo, taken a second or two later, shows the mare reacting to her situation in a typical manner, trying to rebalance herself and slow her forward momentum by throwing her head and neck up and increasing the flexion in the joints of her legs. Note, however, that while she has tightened the flexion of the joints, the legs are folding backward rather than upward. Since she was forehand-heavy when she entered the line (her body was not balanced over her hind legs), it is extremely difficult for her to recover her balance once in the line.

In this same-day photo, we see the mare has learned a lesson about balance, as she enters the line again, carrying herself in a better balance. Her hind legs have become active, engaging with greater energy under her body. This lightens her forehand, allowing her shoulder to lift her forearm up, articulating the knee up. Her back is relaxed, and while she has not quite yet reached the maximally rounded frame that will produce the most notable muscular enhancement of her top line and driving muscles, she is carrying her neck and head with the muscles at the top of her neck, rather than overusing the lower neck muscles as she had been doing in the previous photo.

Trail Work: Topography

Topography means using the physical features and structural relationship of land in developing and training horses. The simple act of riding a horse across a pasture while trailing a cow is a training technique that can address physical, mental, and emotional issues. This book isn't long enough to cover everything about training horses using country, but what it can do is make you aware that a trail ride is seldom just a trail ride for your horse. If you want to be "smarter than the average bear" as a trainer, expand your knowledge of training beyond the arena and learn how topography can be used, like exercise machines at a gym, to build the equine body.

I suppose I could simply state that trail or outside work is a valuable experience in any horse's training program. I could go so far as to say that no horse is truly educated without such training and experience. This is like saying the sun divides the day from the night. This is true, but what is not being said about the sun would also fill not just volumes, but libraries. So it is with training horses by using what nature provides, the land with all of its various questions.

I have for a long time deliberately chosen mustangs for a business in which the primary job of the horses was to be ridden and competed over distances of twenty-five to fifty miles. Why mustangs instead of Arabians, the most popular breed in endurance riding? Because nature and the land is educating the mustang from the time he is born until the time he comes into my hands (I adopt them at 3 years of age, not before) and what nature's terrain teaches them (how to balance and move) is a critically important part of their education as well as an important period of preparation (strengthening and toughening muscles, tendons, hooves, bones, and ligaments) for the job I want him to perform when he is with me. Nature covers a great range of subject matter and what nature has taught them, I don't need to spend time teaching them, so my job is made considerably easier. The early cowboys knew the value of range-raised horses. Today, in small, out-of-the way places with open and accessible land, there are stories of horse trainers, men and women known for their minimum use of words, who still look to the land as a major factor in training horses. It is the type of training referred to in the phrase "A good horse is made with a lot of wet saddle blankets."

The Story of the Flat-Land Horse

When I was a young trainer, I made the mistake of thinking that all horses, no matter what their upbringing, would instinctually know how to go up and/or down a hill. They were, after all, horses, and that's what

horses do, gallop across the land (or so I thought). Then I found an athletic young thoroughbred who was too slow for the racing game for which
he'd been bred. His long, smooth stride and the way he was put together
led me to believe he would be a top candidate for eventing (the three-
phase test of sport horses). He'd already been backed as a part of his
track training, so I spent only thirty days in the arena with him, making
sure I could get the responses I wanted: go when I ask, turn when I say,
stop when I told him to. He was soon performing all of this to my satisfaction, so it was time to move him into the next phase of his education
and conditioning program: take him out on the trail. Bred and raised on
flat land, this horse had never even seen a hill until that first trail ride.

All went extremely well for the first mile because the ground was level.
Then we entered regional park district property. The trail immediately
dropped down a hill at a moderate angle for about three hundred feet into
a gully, then wound its way up the other side. The thoroughbred spread
his legs and froze in his tracks. His reaction was so severe I though he
had seen some wildlife on the opposite side of the hill that had spooked
him. After waiting a bit, I finally persuaded him to move, but he would
only turn in place like a spinning top, or try to run backward the way we
had come. A few minutes became ten, then twenty, then thirty as I tried
to figure out what obviously had my horse near hysteria (he wasn't an
emotional type of thoroughbred, which was one of the things I had liked
about him when I bought him and brought him home with me).

Finally, I decided to dismount and try leading him forward since I
hadn't made any progress with any of the other tactics. I stepped down
and asked him to follow me down the hill. He did so, but his eyes were
huge and his legs trembled with every step. He literally felt his way
down that dirt road inches at a time, on his toes, like a blind man trying
to feel for his footing with every step. I couldn't believe what my eyes
(and the horse) were telling me. A horse who didn't know he could walk
down a hill? Ridiculous maybe, but true nonetheless. It took four trips
(on different days) being led in hand before he would consider trying it
with me in the saddle. Although he became braver and braver (meaning
he was taking normal horse-size strides as he followed me down into the
gulley on our fourth go round), the first time I again asked him to attempt
to handle the terrain with me on his back, he went back to taking six-
inch steps with each foot and I could feel his whole body shaking like
we were in an earthquake. I am happy to report he finally overcame his
fear and turned into the winning event horse I knew he was capable of
becoming, but it was a lesson in assumptions about horses and what was
"natural" to them that I have never forgotten.

Well-trained, arena broke horses are known to perceive simple, harmless manifestations of nature (like rocks, dead logs, hills, and water) with great suspicion, especially when they encounter them in an outdoor setting.

You can strengthen the muscle groups that are responsible for enabling the horse to both collect and extend his body and gaits with graduated hill work. You can teach them to stretch over their top line, accessing their full potential to drive through lifted and lengthened back muscles. You can teach them to sit down, flexing not just their hocks but also all the other hind end joints evenly (see the photos on pages 70 and 71). This will spread the stress of such work evenly throughout all the joints, rather than have it accumulate primarily in one joint, such as stifles or hocks, causing them to fail prematurely. You can do all of that with work over terrain, but you must do it slowly, exercising patience and letting the horse tell you what he can handle and when he can handle it. A horse who doesn't trust his ability to push his weight up an incline will try to hurry his gait. This can become so excessive that some horses will try to gallop up steep inclines. If the distance is not short enough for the horse to outmuscle gravity by pulling with its front end, he may panic and try to turn around, perhaps even fall backward. How can such a situation be avoided in training? By the smarter member of the team making sure they pick and tackle only graduated climbs which are well within what the horse perceives as his limits, then very gradually increasing the steepness and so the degree of difficulty of such assents and descents, as the horse becomes physically stronger. Some young horses, like young men, think of themselves as invincible and act accordingly. This type of horse is even more of a challenge for a trainer because the horse will tend to overestimate his abilities until he learns better. In the meantime, his trainer has to make better decisions for the team, restraining his horse's enthusiasm and tempering it with the knowledge of experience.

Some Facts and a Word of Caution About Hill Work

Horses are designed to push primarily with their hind legs and to carry primarily with their front legs. This being the case, a horse is better designed to climb a hill (push) than descend a hill (carry). If you ride them down a descent in a *free fall*—meaning they descend supporting themselves primarily with their front legs while outrunning gravity in order to stay upright (for an extreme example of this concept, watch the downhill ride in the movie *Man from Snowy River*)—you won't be asking the muscles and joints of the haunches to be doing much work. But the moment you ask the horse to balance and level himself while carrying a rider and descending that same hill, you are going to be requiring the horse's hind end muscles to be doing something they aren't used to doing, especially if the horse is young and undeveloped.

As a trainer, it's your job to improve the horse in a number of ways. You teach him how best to live with humans. You teach him how to use his body in a way that will allow him to carry the weight of a rider without prematurely sacrificing his soundness to that cause. You expand his performance potential by refining his responses to a learned vocabulary of cues or aids and you expand his athleticism by riding him through exercises, which will strengthen his muscles, bones, tendons, ligaments, heart, and lungs.

Now here's the rub: You can only strengthen the horse by regularly taking him to the edge of his fitness level, but you must not cross over that line. If you push the horse beyond the edge of his fitness, you will create more damage to his system than nature can repair within a twenty-four-to forty-eight-hour period. Unfortunately, structural damage at this type of minor level in the horse's body is easily overlooked. If you're watching closely, the horse may give you clues to his situation by a slight shortening of stride, by being just a little stiff at the beginning of his workout, by being a little bit less enthusiastic about his lessons than he was the day before. It is easy to overlook or dismiss such signs and if they are constantly overlooked, the training process, which should be building the horse up, is subtly breaking his systems down instead. It may take a year, or two, or even three or more for these tiny daily or weekly system failures to exhibit themselves in a way that prevents further use or training; lameness, loss of brilliance, sour disposition, saddle fit issues due to uneven muscling, or uneven hoof development—the list goes on.

The process is the same whether the horse is being ridden in an arena or on the trail. The difference is, if you're in an arena and you realize you've pushed your horse a little bit harder than you intended in a given workout or exercise, you can step down immediately and take care of him, ceasing the work and putting him up to rest, allowing mother nature a chance to repair the parts that were stressed. Whether you've ridden your horse one mile or ten, when you realize you've reached the edge of his capacity for that day, you've still got to get him home and it is during the time you are "getting him home" when there is the greatest risk of damage to his body.

If you're conditioning your horse and ride him up a half-mile-long hill and he seems to handle it well, you can expect his hindquarter muscles to become fatigued before you are halfway back down that same hill. Why? Because as I pointed out, the horse is used to pushing, not carrying. As the horse begins to feel the stress of using muscles in a way or to a degree that he is not accustomed to, he will begin to "cheat," letting his weight fall back onto his forehand or positioning himself crookedly relative to the hill, to reduce the stress he feels, at least on one side, temporarily. A horse who resists going straight down an incline, choosing instead to move in a zigzag line from side to side as he descends, or one who, when faced with going down a hill suddenly stops engaging his hind legs under his body and starts instead to move in small shuffling steps, is exhibiting either immediate discomfort or remembered discomfort. In either case, his athletic potential is short-circuited and his muscular development is likely to become one sided and/or unbalanced if he is left to continue in a crooked fashion. A smart trainer will not put his horse in a situation where the horse is being programmed in a negative manner, either physically or mentally, because once programmed into a horse's body and movement pattern, defensive behavior is extremely hard to eradicate.

A young horse shows the lowered head and neck and lengthened top line of a horse, using his body in a productive, physically enhancing frame while ascending a moderate hill.

The same horse demonstrates she has learned the lesson of efficient hill-climbing body mechanics as she successfully tackles a significantly greater challenge in this much steeper assent, by lowering her head and neck even further as a counterbalance to the hill and by correctly increasing the drive from her power source—her hind end—rather than attempting to pull herself up the steep grade with her front end.

In this photo the rider has returned to the lesser challenge of the more moderate hill but increased the demand by asking the mare to trot up the hill while still maintaining good form, driving from her hind end.

A young horse being introduced to descending work lets herself down a moderate hill in a shortened, tentative stride at the walk.

As the mare nears the bottom of the hill, she encounters a training ground pole. The purpose of this pole, placed near the bottom of the grade, is to encourage the horse to extend her stride and carry more of her body weight on her hind legs while still descending the slope without any increase in the speed of her descent.

The much deeper engagement (under the body) of the mare's elevated hind leg, and the lowering of her hindquarters, show the results of this training exercise in the third photo of this series.

Chapter 4

Equitation: Six Deadly Position Faults and How To Fix Them

The Chair Seat

Description: The vertical (non)alignment of the rider's body when mounted puts the rider's foot and leg in front of the torso and ahead of the rider's center of balance (as shown in the photo on the following page).

Cause: This position fault can have a number of causes, including pushing the foot against the stirrup in order to sink the heel lower than the toe; using a defensive riding position when starting young or spooky horses; stiff knee and/or ankle joints in the rider; small hips and tight muscles and ligaments around the hip joint, which make it difficult for a rider to straddle the width of a western saddle comfortably and still allow the legs to "hang" straight down the horse's side; and pinching knees or thighs.

Negative effects: Because the rider's foot is not under his or her body mass, the rider is out of balance with gravity. If the rider's feet are stable in this position, the horse can learn to compensate for the additional weight load this puts on his loins. However, if there is also tension in the rider's hip joints and lower back, the rider's pelvis becomes a driving tool, making the horse want to accelerate (especially when loping) and/or causing them to travel forehand heavy or with a hollow back or both.

To fix: Start by lifting both of your legs forward, completely up off the saddle. Flexing your knees, bring your foot half way up the shoulder of the horse. (Use a calm, quiet horse when first practicing this exercise, or have someone hold the horse while you experiment with finding this new riding position for yourself.) With your leg out of the way in this manner, scoot your seat forward in the saddle, until you are sitting in the middle and not against the cantle. Without tipping your hips either forward or backward, lower your legs one at a time, down the horse's sides. If you can see more than your toe when you glance down over your knee, your foot is still too far forward. Be sure your knee is flexed and your toe is held up as you slowly work to draw your foot back and under your body. Allow your knees to slide down the saddle as you try to slide your feet back under yourself (as shown in the right-hand photo). Make sure to stay firmly seated on your *hip pockets* (think of the back pockets on a pair of jeans) while you work to lengthen your leg and correctly position your foot under your torso. When you put your foot back into the stirrup, be sure the stirrup is adjusted correctly. The length of the stirrup should be set to give the rider's foot support without the rider having to point the toe down in order to make a solid contact with the stirrup tread.

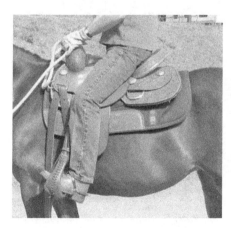 

The rider in a chair seat with her foot and leg in front of the gravitational balance point.

The rider has brought her foot and leg back under her torso, putting herself in better balance on the horse.

Pinching Thighs/Knees

Description: The inner muscles of the rider's thigh are contracted, bringing the thighbone and the knee into strong, continuous contact with the saddle (as shown in the photo on this page).

Cause: This is generally done to increase the rider's feeling of security, especially if a rider's body is not right with gravity (that is, in balance) when she sits on the horse. This pinching or gripping action provides only a temporary feeling of security, because in tightening the thighs against the saddle, the rider destabilizes his or her seat, causing it to rise up, away from the horse's back.

Negative effects: Many horses—especially the hotter breeds like Arabians and quarter horses with a high percentage of thoroughbred blood in their pedigree—are very sensitive to pressure in the region of their back and will both invert (hollow) the back in an attempt to get away from the discomfort of the pinching, and shorten and quicken their gait as a result.

To fix: Lots of work without stirrups, first at walk, then at jog, and finally at lope. Riders can use the scissors leg exercise to loosen the grip in their inner thigh. Here's how: With the feet out of the stirrups, lock the knee joints, then move the entire leg from the hip joint only, taking one foot forward, while the other is drawn backward toward the horse's tail at the same time. Do this without disturbing your seat in the saddle.

This photo shows a rider gripping the saddle with her inner thigh muscles. Note how the contraction has pulled her knee up and the lower leg forward and out of position.

The rider has now relaxed the muscles of her inner thigh and is allowing her leg to lengthen. Looking at the change in the space between her leg and the swell of the saddle as well as the latigo keeper clearly shows the different leg position on the saddle.

Then swap leg positions, drawing the opposite leg forward while taking the formerly forward leg backward toward the horse's tail. Move the legs simultaneously in this exercise, which will work to release a pinching thigh only if the rider moves the leg from the hip joint and does not bend the knee to move the foot. As the tendons and ligaments around the ball-and-socket joint relax and lengthen, the rider's thigh and knee lie against the saddle without tension (as demonstrated in the right-hand photo on the preceding page).

An Arched/Tense Back

Description: The rider's spine is stacked or carried in a distorted S shape between her head and tailbone (as shown in the left-hand photo on this page).

Cause: Tension in the muscles of the lower back and in the area of the chest hold the body in this stressful, unnatural position, both on the ground and in the saddle.

Negative effects: As a result of tension, the angle of the pelvis will not allow the rider's seat bones to settle into the deepest part of the saddle, so the rider does not have a solid base of support with the security it should provide, nor can she use her seat as a communication tool. With this amount of tension in the back, the rider will be forced to grip with her legs for security. When the leg is tied up in acting as a

This rider's back shows the "hollow" appearance of a tense, arched back and is an example of an improperly positioned pelvis.

The rider has adjusted her seat, bringing her seat bones into the deepest part of her saddle, while using her core muscles to hold her pelvis in a vertical position, causing her back to flatten.

gripping/security device, its ability to serve as an independent communication tool to the horse is distinctly reduced or even eliminated entirely.

To fix: Sit in the saddle with your feet out of your stirrups. Place one hand at the small of your back and one hand over your lower abdomen. Think of letting your belly button drop backward toward your spine until you feel your back flatten under your hand. Try to produce this straight-back posture (as shown in the right-hand photo on the preceding page) without leaning your shoulders back. Use only the muscles of your back and abdomen to change the position of your pelvis, making it perpendicular to the ground. Try doing this exercise off the horse while watching yourself in a mirror. This can be a tremendous help because if you have this posture fault, your brain will believe your back is straight even when you can easily see in the mirror that it is curved. Therefore, when you first begin to correct this fault, your brain will try to make you believe you are "round backed." The mirror and your hand in the small of your back will let you know that, in fact, your back is straight. This *distorted kinesthetic sense* (a belief that something is so, which is not) will gradually diminish as you practice your improved position and should be gone entirely after three to four weeks of continuous practice.

A Collapsed Rib Cage

Description: The rider's rib cage is contracted or collapsed on one side (as shown in the left-hand photo on the following page). One shoulder is closer to the ride's hip on the same side, creating the appearance of a curl or a C curve when the rider's body is viewed from the rear while sitting on the horse.

Cause: An unbalanced unilateral tightening or overdevelopment of the muscles on one side of the rider's back.

Negative effects: This crooked; lateral torso position unlevels the rider's pelvis, making sitting in balance in the saddle impossible. The rider will experience difficulty keeping both feet in the stirrups, always losing contact with one stirrup or feeling as though the stirrup on the collapsed side is too short. This sided rider posture unbalances the horse, causing him to compensate for the rider by overdeveloping the muscles on one side of his body and preventing the horse from having any chance at straightening his body. Through time, this unequal muscle development leads to saddle fit issues, hoof balance and soundness issues, and back soreness and can create lead problems at lope.

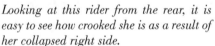

Looking at this rider from the rear, it is easy to see how crooked she is as a result of her collapsed right side.

Stretching the right side of her rib cage has allowed this rider to square her seat on her horse and level her shoulders.

To fix: One simple way to begin to fix this fault is for the rider to extend her hand and arm straight up over her head on the curved side, holding it there as the horse walks or jogs, while removing her foot from the stirrup on the same side and dropping her leg toward the ground. This stretches the rib cage and levels, at least momentarily, the pelvis, allowing the rider to sit squarely in the saddle (as the shown in the right-hand photo on this page).

Elevated Heel and Dropped Toe

Description: In this physical alignment of the rider's foot, the toe is closer to the ground than the rider's heel when the foot is in the stirrup (as shown in the left-hand photo on the following page).

Cause: This can result from stirrups that are too long, stiff ankles, misunderstanding about how and why the rider's foot should make and keep contact with the stirrup, or improper use of or positioning of the foot and leg when delivering leg aids to the horse.

When the toe of the foot is carried below the level of the heel, the ankle becomes tense.

Raising the toe and dropping the heel will better allow the ankle to fulfill its purpose as a shock-absorbing joint.

Negative effects: Stiffens or locks the ankle, taking away the joint's ability to function as a shock absorber. Tends to loosen the rider's seat in the saddle and throw the rider's body behind or ahead of the motion of the horse.

To fix: Adjust the stirrup length so the stirrup supports the bottom of your foot when your toe is actively being lifted upward slightly toward your knee. Keep the pressure on your foot distributed over the entire surface of the ball of the foot or toward the big toe edge of your foot, never toward the little toe (outward) edge of the foot. Practice stretches like the *skier's stretch:* With both your hands against a solid surface, like a flat wall, walk your feet backward until your body is at about a 45-degree angle to the wall, keep your spine, pelvis, and legs in a straight line, and press your heels to the floor. This stretches and lengthens your Achilles tendons, promoting the flexibility necessary to drop your heel below your toe when your foot is in the stirrup (as shown in the photo on the right).

Misaligned and Tense Hands, Wrists, and Arms

Description: The misalignment of the rider's hands, wrists, forearm, elbow, and upper arms relates to the reins, bit, and the horse's mouth (as shown in the photos on the following page).

Cause: Reins too long. Rider balancing on the reins. Tension in the rider's hands, wrists, and/or arms, shoulders, and chest. The rider may

Rider's wrists broken inward.

Rider's wrists broken outward and elbows lifted away from her sides.

lack understanding of and education about the various actions of the bit in the horse's mouth and how the reins cause these effects through the bit. There may also be a lack of knowledge about how and when to adjust rein length quickly and effectively.

Negative effects: Any excess tension (stiffness) in the rider's fingers, hands, wrists, arms (either lower or upper), shoulders, and chest has the result of sending unwanted vibrations into the bit and consequently into the mouth of the horse, causing the horse to defend himself from the discomfort by tensing his jaw, neck, and body respectively. This tensing in the horse detracts from his ability to relax and perform to the extent of his athletic capacity. It may also cause the horse to toss his head or pull against his bit and the rider's hand.

To fix: In order to have quiet hands, the rider's seat must first be balanced and solid. Doing *shoulder roll exercises* to release excess tension in the area of the shoulders will help your arms hang at your sides in a relaxed manner. Simply lift and roll both shoulders at the same time in

Correct rein, hand, wrist, and forearm alignment, viewed from the front.

Correct rein, hand, wrist, and forearm alignment, viewed from the side.

a circular motion, first up and backward, and then downward and for-ward. Keep the forearm, wrist, and hands in correct alignment (as shown in the bottom photos on the preceding page). Also, keeping the hands positioned so the thumb is on the top of the fist will help keep your hand and wrist relaxed. Focus on the ability to use the muscles of the fingers and thumb independently, without inadvertently tensing the muscles in your wrists, or freezing or stiffening them.

Chapter 5

Dressing the Role

with Suzanne Drnec

Clothes and Image

While there is wisdom in the admonition about not judging a book by its cover, there can be little doubt that cowboys and cowgirls have a distinctive style or look, one that easily distinguishes them from a group of traders on the floor of the New York Stock Exchange, for instance. The clothing that is most often associated with today's working cowboy has strong roots in history and practicality, while the fashions of the show pen rider, who participates in classes such as horsemanship and pleasure, strongly suggest a splashier Hollywood influence, one that first appeared on the public stage in the 1940s and 1950s with the legendary singing cowboys Roy Rogers and Gene Autry.

While it is always good advice to buy the best-quality items you can afford, whether tack or clothing, no matter what your style, a good western wardrobe shouldn't cost a mint, especially if you plan ahead and shop carefully. On the show stage it's vitally important that no detail is overlooked, either in your performance or in your turnout. If you want to win, you want your horse well schooled and groomed to perfection, and you want to look like a winner.

Remember, your choices must be legal and appropriate for the class and level of competition. Gymkhanas (see chapter 8), as well as team

Hobby Horse

Form-fitting show apparel should flatter horse and rider in color and design.

penning (see chapter 9), are events in which attire is much less formal than what's required at top-level show competitions.

- Your equipment must satisfy the rules of the association or club you show with, so become familiar with your rulebook and don't lose a prize just because you didn't know.

- Because you're being judged on how you look as well as how you perform, there's no sense in not looking your best. Wisely planning a good show wardrobe will not only help you make a good impression but will also give you confidence each time you enter the arena.

What You Can Expect to Pay

If you're a new rider with no wardrobe and you want to show, plan on investing close to $1,000 for chaps (leather leg coverings), hat, show blanket, and assorted clothes. This will get you a quality western wardrobe, suitable for showing competitively at local and regional-level shows. Although fashion in the horse show world certainly changes, it doesn't do so at the rate of street apparel. Good basic hats and chaps will be fashionable for many years. With reasonable care and if you have a semi-consistent body weight, they shouldn't need replacing frequently. Show clothing fashions have a lifecycle of several years from the time something new hits the world shows, then trickles down to local or regional level shows. So figure that you're investing in clothing that should be useful in your wardrobe for three or four years, then budget and invest accordingly.

Consider this: If you show once a month for four years, the difference between a terrific $1,000 wardrobe and an average-at-best $500 bunch of clothes is about $10 per show. Isn't it worth the extra ten bucks to look like a winner? Great performances don't happen accidentally. They're scripted, rehearsed, and polished long before they're presented to an audience or a judge. Both color and style play an important part in making you and your horse stand out from the crowd. Keeping your riding skills and your horse's best traits in mind, your job will be to decide how you can best use color and style to highlight your show-ring performance and your personality.

Good show clothing is not an expense; it's an investment in your success. Consider the classes you're likely to show in for the next year, and then choose the clothes you'll need. Keep an eye on color and style and add pieces that mix and match to build a flexible, versatile wardrobe.

Making Your Color Choices Work for You

Color plays an important role in the impression you make in the show ring. You must flatter your horse at the same time you try to look unique—quite a trick when there are twenty sorrel horses with riders in black chaps loping around together.

Before you choose colors, keep in mind that the color of your horse affects the overall picture much more than your little face does. Don't ever choose something you don't like, but dress for your horse as well as for yourself, because very little of your coloring shows in the pen, compared to the acre of horse you're riding! When it comes to color, trust your instincts, start simple, and study the impression color creates in the show ring before you start spending.

In general, horses are either *redheads* (sorrel, chestnut, red roan, rose gray, dun), which look especially nice with softer earth-toned shades of sand, rust, brown, peach, and almost any green tone; or they're *brunettes* (bay, black, white, most grays—horses with brown, black, or white hair), which can wear bright jewel-toned colors like red, blue, purple, and greens. *Neutral-color* horses (including palominos, buckskins, and grullas) can use either earth-toned or jewel-toned accents, depending on the rider's preferences, horse's coat color, and the horse's markings.

Some horses, including appaloosas, pintos, and paints, are a little harder to classify. If your horse has more than 50 percent body white,

Enhancing Your Conformation

Dark colors minimize. Light colors emphasize. Smaller-patterned or vertical-striped fabrics reduce and lengthen; large, bold stripes or horizontal designs compress the eye, creating the illusion of widening the space (and the part of your body) they cover.

If you have large hips or thighs and want to minimize them, try a dark chap color, with a vertical-patterned dark vest to minimize your middle. Top it off with a light hat to visually draw the observer's eye upward and create the illusion of height in your upper body.

If your top half is large, try to keep layers—a lapel, ties, and collars—to a minimum on your chest; instead, go for a color blend at the waist.

If you're tall, a darker hat visually compresses you a little, especially with a darkish outfit below it.

If you are petite, use sharp color contrast between chaps and tops, and emphasize accessories—bolder ties or a little more jewelry.

Any figure will look trimmer if you try to make everything—chaps, belt, vest/jacket, shirt—come together at your natural waist instead of at your hips. No color or style will erase your figure flaws, but careful choices can emphasize your good points and minimize your weaknesses. Trends come and go, but good taste is always in style. Study breed journals and other magazines to see what look is in style in your area. Better yet, bring a camera to a few shows like those you'll be competing in and snap a few reminders of what you did or didn't like.

If you would like to preview outfit colors on a variety of horses, check out the interActiv feature on the Hobby Horse Web site (www.hobbyhorseinc.com). It's a fun way to get an idea of how great, or how average, a color combination might be on your horse.

consider the brunette/jewel-toned colors to contrast with your horse's white coat, and avoid a dreary sand-chaps-on-an-almost-white-horse combination. If your colorful horse has less than 50 percent body white, use his primary coat color as the determining factor. For example, a minimal white sorrel overo paint would probably look best in the redhead/earth-toned colors.

If you ride several horses or aren't sure what color horse you may be showing, consider the versatile blue/green color range. From the palest mint to the deepest forest green, these colors look great on almost any horse color, and also carry well from a distance in the show ring. Picture a beautiful teal green shirt with a matching saddle blanket on a sorrel horse and a bay—it's a winning picture either way.

Starting at the Top: Hats

Hats, like chaps, were originally a clothing item whose primary purpose was protection, but on today's western scene, hats add flair and character to your wardrobe, say something about who you are, and/or finish off your look. Your hat should fit comfortably and stay on in a stiff breeze, and it should flatter your facial structure, as well as punctuating the rest of your outfit. Hats also declare whether you're a real horseman or a wannabe. Subtle differences in quality, shape, and maintenance make your western hat an absolute billboard for the person under the brim. Hat styles often vary with different types of events.

Western hats—which come in two basic types, felt or straw—can probably trace their history all the way back to the Mongols, whose horsemen's costumes included large hats. More recently, history shows us examples of riders wearing large hats with the Spanish and Mexican sombreros.

Hat Material: Felt versus Straw

Cowboy hats come in a wide variety of shapes and sizes, the height of the crown and the width of the brim marking a hat as distinctive as the shape of the crown. Although sizes, colors, shapes, and trims can vary tremendously, hats appropriate for western competition fall into two groups: felt and straw. Safety helmets are legal for use in most western events but are not often seen in the show pen, since manufacturers have yet to made a western safety hat that combines both impact resistance and a classic western silhouette.

Felt Hats

Felt hats are made from a blend of various animal fur fibers. Making felt for a hat is similar to accidentally washing a wool sweater in your washing machine: fibers are agitated under heat and pressure, and the tiny barbs that exist along the animal fur fibers lock or *felt* together. Prestige western felt hats contain a high percentage of fur fibers like beaver, which have many more hooks than, say, wool, so the resulting felt is much denser, smoother, and more moisture repellent than a wool hat. Better felt hats really are better—they hold their shape longer, repel dirt and moisture, and look, simply, more expensive.

Felt hat quality is denoted by Xs—the higher the percentage of expensive fur in the felt blend, the more Xs the hat's interior sweatband displays as a badge of quality. Beware, though: X designations aren't regulated, so one manufacturer's 20X may be the quality of another company's 7X. Similar hats from the same manufacturer can have tremendous variation in smoothness, body, and integrity—try several if you can to compare.

Straw Hats

Straw hats are rarely made from straw these days—they're almost always constructed from finely processed paper fibers that are woven into a variety of hat styles. Straw hats, whose relative quality is usually denoted by Xs (or sometimes by stars), are more expensive when they're made from very tiny fibers that take longer to weave. Different designs are woven into the crown to create decorative vents, which not only add interest to the hat but also make for built-in comfort in hot weather.

All straw hats have a wire woven into the outside edge of the brim to allow for gentle hand shaping, but the crowns are shaped and shellacked at the factory and can't easily be modified, so buy what you like and don't plan to change your straw's shape much. Straws can be cleaned by gently wiping them with a damp cloth, but once sweat stains show on the outside of your straw, it's time for a new one. Straws are always considered more casual than felts, and are worn primarily in spring and summer or in humid climates.

Choosing the Right Hat

A good hat is an important investment. Hats can vary in price from around $40 for a decent straw to $1,000 for a 100X Stetson. When shopping for a hat, note the following considerations.

Color

A black hat always looks nice with black chaps, but it can cast a harsh, unflattering shadow over the rider's face. Pale neutral felt hats highlight your face. Neutral hats in cool, grayish shades like platinum or crystal look best worn with bright jewel-toned colors like purple or red; neutrals in warm golden tones like buckskin or sand look best with earthy shades—rust, beiges, and so on. Brightly colored hats are out of fashion these days in the show pen.

Style

A basic cattleman's crown with a 4-inch brim is pretty standard, but women with smaller faces and children should certainly consider having their brim trimmed by at least 1/4 inch. Full 4-inch brims are designed for men, and often make smaller people look like mushrooms. A little judicious trimming and shaping can ensure your hat will flatter you.

Service After the Sale

It's imperative to buy your western hats from an experienced retailer. Don't trade at a store that isn't serious enough about hats to offer shaping, trimming, and expert consultation. Spending a few more dollars to have your hat professionally shaped and fitted is the way to go, whether you have a great western store in your area, shop at the trade show of a major event, or discuss your exact needs over the phone with the resident hat expert from a store far away.

When selecting a hat, keep in mind the overall look you will achieve when you wear it.

Tips About Your Outfit Topper

Keep the following in mind as you shop for a hat.

- Hat shape, color, and size affect how you look.

- Tall riders can shorten their look with a dark hat.

- Short riders can lengthen their look with a pale hat.

- Overhead lighting exaggerates hat shadows on your face.

- Certain outfits (such as the one exhibited by the rider in the photo) or activities beg for a particular hat. Find out what type of hat goes with what type of activity and compare hat styles before you buy.

Caring for Your Hat

Even the finest hats look horrible if you don't take care of them. Learn how to put your hat on, never touching the delicate brim, and also how to clean it with a curved-handled soft hat brush. Invest in a good case, and never leave your hat in a hot car or a horse trailer in a plastic bag— it will warp in the heat and look like a tortilla chip.

Blouses, Tops, and Shirts

Historically, cowboy shirts were made of good-quality material, primarily virgin wool or cotton denim, and displayed basic lines. Working cowboy clothes have changed little over the years. Fine-check plaids were common, as were neutral browns. Protection from the elements and the need for freedom of action were the two most important governing factors in the clothing's design. Jackets were sometimes made of a canvas ducking, which provided a long-lived and highly serviceable garment.

In today's show pen atmosphere, your torso topper sets the pace for the impression you convey, whether sophisticated, casual, or trendy. Your upper-body garments are the fashion foundation of your western show outfit

Not up for auditioning as history's infamous au naturel rider, Lady Godiva, or a spot on the Chippendale staff? Then you'll want to cover the top half of your body with something that's attractive (from a distance), adds deliberate color to the horse/rider presentation, and allows you to perform your job comfortably. Choices range from the ridiculously simple (a basic cotton shirt for a showman) to the sublime (a rhinestone-encrusted Super Slinky for a woman's dazzling presentation in pleasure futurities). You can also wear your "basic black" top under a favorite vest at weekend events.

Show shirts should be big enough in the shoulders for athletic comfort, but trim enough through the waist to stay tucked in without bunching. Sleeves need to be long enough to pass your wrist bone when you have your elbow flexed while riding. Traditional shirts should be 100 percent cotton to support SST (that's show starch technology), achieved by asking your cleaners for military starch so that your shirt will resist billowing even during the fastest rides.

For Men and Boys

Men and boys choose menswear-inspired shirts for their show wardrobes, searching near and far for fabrics that the other guys might not already have. Shop western stores and catalogs as well as department stores for candidates, including bold solids; plaids with a bright base color like orange, red, purple, or green; and small checks that appear almost solid from a distance. Color-block shirts are regaining some of their popularity, and the always correct look for any cowboy, event, or level of competition is the classic white shirt worn with a brightly patterned tie. Snaps are out in the show ring today, but button-down collars will make tie-taming a breeze.

For Women and Girls

For women and girls, there are two basic choices for today's show look: dressy blouses or slinky tops. Slinky tops (form-fitted stretch blouses with long sleeves and high fitted collars) are a popular purchase, and legal for nearly all disciplines. Traditional blouses are a great look for many riders who want to avoid the expense of a vest or a jacket. This is especially true for riders who show in events like reining or cutting where freedom of movement of the rider's arms is paramount.

Pleated-front tuxedo shirts are best packed away to await a revival. Women's blouses may be cotton, starched up to mimic the professional sil-houette of the men, or a drapey fabric like silk or rayon that has fluid movement in motion. Because a trim side silhouette is paramount in the ring, many women's blouses will need tailoring at the waist, perhaps with fitted darts added under the bust. Many types of "slinkies" are intended to be layered under other garments and are too thin to make an appropri-ate show garment by themselves. If you don't have the body of a sixteen-year-old gymnast, what may look great as you stand in front of your mirror can go south in a hurry by the time you climb on your horse. Gravity likes to pull everything down, as your chaps, pants, and belt push everything up, creating a war zone at your waistline. It is a wise woman who test-drives her slinky choice in a saddle before she ventures into the ring.

For layering, slinky tops made from a nylon/Lycra blend are softer and less supportive than those made from thicker-ribbed acetate/Lycra. But you'll pay a few dollars more for the firmer models. If you want sleek good looks *and* carefree comfort in a top that "holds your own," look to knitted fabrics that have stretch and firmness. Do remember that this type of show top will retain more body heat than a thin slinky, but it will still be cooler than a light top with a vest, for example. You'll find these firmer Super Slinkies make a great show garment because they control your midriff but let you perform the most amazing stunts (like heaving your show saddle up on your horse!) in Lycra-clad comfort. They'll fit and feel like an athlete's leotard.

Care tip: All stretch tops should be gently hand-washed and air-dried to preserve the shape and stretchiness of the fabric.

Fashionable Details

Fashionable details give clothes character. Men should steer clear of all but the most traditional cut in shirts for the show ring: band collars, contrasting cuffs, and other fancy touches are best reserved for a big night out on the town. Women, however, have more choices than ever in trims that set the tone for their outfits. Fabrics range from the stretchy, sporty look of slinkies to richly textured velvets, laces, and brocades.

Consider designs that carry well from a distance: embroidered trims, bold sleeve details, appliquéd (sewn-on) suede and leather, and, of course, rhinestones and studs twinkling on everything. More is more for today's show girls.

- Show shirts should combine with your other clothing and horse color to create a pleasant color scheme.

- Layered or worn alone, show shirts should create a trim, smooth silhouette that allows for freedom of movement.

- Show shirts should capture your personality and help you convey an impression of confidence.

- Show shirts must fit when you're in action. This means extra sleeve length, trim and tucked-in torsos, and proportionate collars.

- Tame your top by tucking the tails inside your undies, pinning the shirt front to your pants under your belt buckle, or for the ladies, attaching a panty bottom.

- Women should carefully choose foundation garments to support, firm, and flatter their figures.

- Avoid slinky tops on nonslinky bodies: layer vests or jackets over thin tops, or find power-stretch fabrics for flattering all-in-one looks.
  Two more pieces of advice on shirts:

- **Guys:** Dress up your look with button-down classic shirts featuring small embroidered logos and trim shapes.

- **Gals:** Look for guy-style cottons for casual classes or dressy textiles in fitted fancy blouses.

Vests and Jackets

Vests (shown in the photo on this page) are as much a part of the cowboy persona as they are an important part of the wardrobe in today's competitive show environment. Vests can completely change the personality of your presentation and add versatility to your wardrobe.

Jackets (or blazers), shown in the photo on the following page, are part of the standard show uniform for showmanship and longe line classes these days and a nice option in riding classes as well. If you can only afford one piece, go for a short jacket that you can wear with show pants for halter classes, and with chaps for riding.

Blazers—jackets that are longer than your hip bones—are a fashion fatality when riding, because they simply bunch up around your hips and make you look like a pile of laundry. Blazers and tunic tops (full-length zippered tops that can be worn tucked in for riding events or tails out for halter) are the preferred look in showmanship classes at quarter horse and stock breed shows now.

An important question is, "When should I choose a vest instead of a jacket or a blazer?" If you compete a few times a year at club-level

An amateur showmanship exhibitor sports a nicely tailored vest over her slinky, giving her a trim, attractive look.

Halter exhibitors often choose a classic blazer for their show presentations. Paired with slim-fitting pants, this is a winning look at any size show.

shows, a vest that you can wear over a variety of tops for different looks will trim up your figure, add color or texture to your look, or simply make for a change of pace from blouses. Leather vests with rhinestone trims are popular, but you might look overdressed at a small, casual schooling show.

A vest is usually more casual than a jacket or a blazer. It allows you freedom of movement in your arms—an important consideration in classes like reining and trail, or if you're riding a young horse two-handed. In addition, vests can slightly insulate your upper body in chilly indoor arenas, yet allow body heat to dissipate through the arms and open necklines if you're showing in hot or humid weather. Vests should be long enough to cover at least the top edge of your waistband at your center back when you are mounted. Otherwise your shirt may work its way out as you ride. Armholes should be fairly snug and fitted. Most fashion vests are made to be worn loose and hang open—they never look smooth buttoned up, so invest in a garment designed to fit while you're riding.

In fitting jackets and blazers, a tapered body and lots of sleeve length are necessary—don't let those wrist bones and Rolexes peek out! Vest-length hems are usually best for short jackets, and blazer hems should be proportionate to the wearer's height: taller people can wear longer blazers without looking overwhelmed by fabric. Sleeve trims add interest in

Flattering Your Figure

To flatter your figure, keep the following tips in mind:

- If you're short, look for a vertical pattern to elongate your figure.

- Thinner fabrics add less bulk to your silhouette than quilted or tapestry materials.

- Princess-line seams (curved panels fitting over the bust) fit better than simple darts.

- Full-figured women usually prefer classic styles with simple geometric designs.

- Minimize your waistline with clothes that blend, rather than contrast, with your pants or chaps color.

- Try on show apparel with the rest of your show outfit and your hat. Everything makes you look fat when you try it on over a sweatshirt!

- Avoid delicate fabrics like lightweight satin or embroidered chiffon—they abrade badly at the sides and are often an expensive disappointment.

- Don't settle for quality that is not at least as good as national brands of women's wear in department stores—show clothes take a lot of abuse and also need to clean easily.

the arena, and can be placed all over: on shoulders or cuffs or perhaps tied in with yokes on the bodice of the garment.

Vest, jacket, and blazer fabrics range from the simple to the sublime, from denim to tapestries, wool to fine leather. They can be trimmed with anything from pretty buttons to faux fur collars, and decorations include appliqués, embroidery, rhinestones, nail heads (metal rhinestones), and contrasting fabrics. Necklines may be V-shaped, rounded, or high in design, or form novelty shapes including tulips and stars, with or without collars in mandarin, shirt, and band styles. Popular closures include buttons, toggles, and zippers in single- and double-breasted styles. Try several different garments to see what looks best on you.

Pants

In the show ring, you'll see everything from faded, worn jeans to beautifully tailored slacks—it seems like anything goes. For men, the standard, always correct look is snugly fitted starched classic jeans under chaps. Fuller jeans are a great fashion look, but their roomier leg and thigh usually make them bunch and wrinkle under chaps. Guys, unless you are fuller cut, traditional cowboy jeans will fit more smoothly and be more comfortable under snug chaps. For showmanship and halter, you can use your same heavily starched (but not heavily faded) jeans with a crisp shirt at small shows, but in serious competition consider pleated khakis or denims and a sport coat to dress up your basic shirt.

Classic jeans can work on women, especially if you wear black chaps with black pants, but the pockets, yokes, and heavy seams on jeans make for a bumpy, bulky fit under chaps, especially Ultrasuede models. Also, women's fashion jeans that make you look like a model when you're standing tend to ride up when you're in the saddle, allowing bunches of fabric to ooze out the front of your chaps. Fashion jeans can also do strange things in the rise when you sit in a saddle that makes them mighty annoying for active riding. The best choice under chaps are fitted, plain (no yokes or pockets) polyester pants with just a hint of stretch. Your "hindquarters" will always look smaller with pants that exactly match the color of your chaps. If you do have colored chaps, though, you may have to have the pants made in that special shade of persimmon or azure. Try to find a sturdy stretch fabric and have the pants sewn with a side zipper to keep them flatter across the tummy. Always buy extra fabric—chances are you'll never find it again. Consider having three pairs of pants made: one to ride in (these will suffer some abrasion on the seat and legs) along with a pair for halter events, and a spare pair for when the dry cleaners lose a pair.

Girl's and women's show pants are available from several manufacturers, but if you can't find the pants you need and don't want to go through the hassle of having pants custom-made, consider English breeches. There's a wide range of colors available, and the great stretch fabrics will fit smoothly and trimly under your chaps: just pull your boots over the bottom edge of the breeches and zip your chaps over the whole shebang for great riding comfort, often at a very comfortable price. Shopping tip: Be sure the breeches have belt loops wide enough to accommodate your western belt.

For women and girls in showmanship, it's important to have the look of fitted, slightly flared, smooth-waisted pants that are hemmed long enough to cover your boots when you jog with your horse. Determine the proper hem length by pinning or basting the hem, then walk and jog around the house with your boots on to see if your pants ride up your boot legs. Sew small drapery weights in the heel hems of your show pants, or try offset hems that are longer over the heel if you can't get the look you want.

Some show girls wear pleated pants for less formal halter events, but be sure the fuller silhouette is flattering to you with the jacket, blazer, or vest you plan to wear. Sometimes these trousers make a short handler look like a melting pile of fabric, so be sure the look suits you. If you do wear trousers, remember to buy them miles too long so you can "starch and stack" the excess length: make a series of small, rippling pleats from your instep up the first few inches of your boot top. These pants would offend a tailor, but it's popular in the show pen to look like you suddenly expect to grow about six inches and don't want to be caught with your pants too short.

Chaps

Chaps are leather leggings that cover the rider's leg from the ankle to the hip or from mid-calf to the hip. Initially they were used to protect the legs. The original Mexican term for this piece of cowboy clothing was actually *armas,* meaning armor. Nowadays many riders use them for better grip in the saddle and to prevent chafing of their leg, as well as using the more flamboyant styles of chaps—such as those made of fur or angora goatskin (as shown in the photo on the following page)—as a costume piece. The *shotgun* or *closed-leg* style of chaps, with or without fringe, is the type most commonly seen today, especially in the show pen. This was also the style most preferred by old cowmen, since it was light in weight as well as warm and rainproof. Because oiled leather has a tendency to become stiff and uncomfortable in cold weather, fur chaps, which shed rain without being oiled, were the popular choice of riders who lived and worked in cold or damp climates.

Chaps made from bearskin were also common in the early days. With the additional cushioning offered by the hair, these types of chaps offered a great deal of protection from the bruises that could occur when rider and horse had a difference of opinion, resulting in the rider being

Photo by Hobby Horse

Chaps cover more than half of your body, so they must fit smoothly, with minimal wrinkling and have a trim look at the waist.

A "Mounted Shooting" contestant sports a pair of historical chaps as a part of his historically accurate outfit.

"Batwing" chaps can create quite an impression.

rubbed up against fence posts in a breaking pen. Another version of chaps, called bat-wing chaps, were worn by riders in wild west shows of the past, and are seen today primarily in the rodeo arena.

For the show rider, chaps (shown in the photo on the preceding page) are the most important element of a winning western wardrobe. They cover more than half of your body and set the tone for color and style that the rest of your ensemble should complement. Your chaps should be the most flattering garment that you own, as they'll very likely be one of the most expensive! But, like just the right show saddle, chaps are an investment that will last for years and enhance your performance every time you enter the show pen.

Deciding Whether You Need Chaps

Does everyone who shows in western classes need chaps? No. A few breeds of horses are shown with western tack but chaps optional. Chaps may also be optional in some local shows and, surprisingly, in NRHA reining competitions. Reining and cutting horse riders may wear a shortened version of the classical chap, called *chinks* (as shown in the photo on the following page). This style of chaps was originally popular with the cowhands in California and Nevada since they were lightweight and much cooler in hot weather.

Short chaps, known as chinks.

For most western show events, a perfectly fitted pair of shotgun chaps should be your goal. Your chaps should make you look slim, feel good, and ride with confidence—which won't happen if they don't fit flawlessly. Show chaps should hang snugly off your waist, not your hips, and should cover some or all of your pants belt when you are mounted. They should fit smoothly through the thigh and hip, with almost no gapping at the front of your thigh. Show chaps should start to zip up high to reduce gapping—picture your zippers starting on the outside lower edge of your jeans pocket—and those zippers should run not down the side of your leg, nor the back, but halfway between those two points. Show chaps should be fitted to the knee with slight ease for comfort, then flare to fit smoothly over your boot tops with no twist to the leg. Your show chaps must be long enough to cover your boot heel when you are in the saddle.

What to Look For

Chap style and construction will vary with the chap maker's experience and sense of style, but look for the following:

- **Heavy shaped yokes and cuffs:** Yokes around your waist reinforce the chaps, minimize stretching, and add a decorative effect. Yoke designs should sandwich the top edge of the outside zipper too, because this point receives tremendous strain. Cuffs add weight to the bottom of your chaps and help them fit tidily around your foot in the stirrup.

- **Thigh reinforcements:** The long, curving expanse of the chap's upper leg is susceptible to stretching and should have a second layer of material sewn to it to minimize stretch. This reinforcement is invisible when sewn to the inside of the chap leg; why many chap makers put it on top of the leg to create an unsightly stripe around the thigh is a mystery.

- **Quality components:** Insist on brass (golden), not aluminum (silver-colored), zippers for long life. All buckles, D rings, and other hardware should be sturdy and attractive.

- **Thoughtful construction:** While synthetic suede is perfect throughout the piece, natural hides have stronger and weaker spots. Leather chaps must be carefully laid out and cut to maximize more attractive leather for the yokes, cuffs, and outer legs, with fuzzier or softer parts of the hide used under the rider's thigh or in the lower leg. Of course, all chap hides should be of excellent quality and large enough to eliminate holes and excessively weak spots from the finished chaps.

Expect to spend several hundred dollars for a great pair of chaps—and consider your needs before you go chap shopping. Though chaps come in many materials, colors, and trim combinations, basic black with fringe is far and away the most common purchase. If your budget dictates only one pair of chaps, put your money into a flawless fit rather than silver accents or exotic leathers. Chaps will last for many years (providing your weight stays within about a twenty-pound range) and it's well worth it to buy quality basics rather than cheap, trendy chaps. Second-hand chaps are also often a bargain, again provided they fit you like that proverbial glove.

Boots

Boots and hat are the two items a real cowboy would never be without. Whether you choose an exotic leather in a wild color, or simple boots that can carry you from the grocery store to the show ring, the shape and detailing of western boots add spice to your overall outfit and help make a personal statement. Calfskin is the leather most commonly used for working boots, while ostrich and other exotic leathers are frequently found in dress boots.

Western boots come with varying heel heights and shapes. The high, angled heels frequently seen on boots of the past were thought to provide safety to the wearer, ensuring the foot wouldn't slip through the stirrup. Today's boots offer a much greater variety of heel shapes and sizes, and knowledgeable riders make their choice based on the jobs they perform and their personal comfort.

Boot making today has become an art form. One only needs to look at ads in magazines such as *Cowboys & Indians* and *American Cowboy*, to see a beautiful array of stunningly crafted footwear in the western style and tradition.

In the show ring, only the toe of your boot will be seen when you ride, so you'll save money by selecting show boots that are sensible and simple, which also means you can afford to have a second pair in a different color choice.

Think about how your boot will look peeking out from under your chaps, through your wide stirrup, and next to your horse's shoulder, then choose something classic that will fill your needs. Coordinate your boot tone to your chaps or your horse's shoulder color by either buying the correct color boots or having a shoe repair shop dye an existing pair of boots. Make sure you keep extra dye for touch-ups.

A basic *roper-style boot* (semi-rounded toe with low tops) with leather soles is the all-around best bet for showing. They are relatively inexpensive, are safe in your stirrups, and fit great under the slim leg of your chaps. Ropers are also the most popular style of boot on the market, so there are a tremendous variety of colors, leathers, and prices. Moderate roper heels are also comfortable to walk in, an important feature for those who show in halter or showmanship.

Lacer boots are our second choice for show boots, but remember to remove the kiltie (fringed panel at the bottom of the laces) to eliminate bulk under the south edge of your chaps. You can spend a ton of money on fancy custom boots. Many of these boots verge on being works of art and some, depending on the maker, are highly collectable items, but buying them for daily wear would be a waste. If you have the type of flamboyant personality that would love to be expressed in "wearable art" footwear, at least save them for party time. Of course, no matter what you spend for boots, they should be freshly shined with good shoe polish and lots of elbow grease for each show day, and dusted with a dry, clean cloth before each class.

Accessories

In the past, the differences in climate dictated cowboy fashions and accessories to a great extent. An experienced cowhand could often tell which part of the country a rider was from by the clothes he wore.

Cuffs, Hatbands, Buckles, and Conchos

- **Leather cuffs:** Used to protect the arms when knocking limbs off brush, and the like (as shown in the photo on this page). Popular especially in the southwest, but only seen in the competition arena today in mounted shooting or in parades.

- **Hatbands:** Worn more in the northwest than in the south, the most popular ones are varicolored and braided from horsehair.

- **Belt buckles:** The most important ornament worn by cowboys both past and present, they are often referred to as "horse jewelry."

  Western belt buckles come in an endless variety of shapes and sizes, but the best buckle to wear in the show ring is always the buckle you just won. There is the "trophy" type buckle (large oval or rectangular buckle with figures and/or lettering) or the smaller three-piece set, a buckle, loop, and tip fitted to a tapered belt and often seen both in the show pen and the "real world" as well.

  Buckles with prongs sometimes lay flatter than those with tongues. The buckle should, of course, always be proportionate to the wearer. If you're fashion conscious, you will allow the width of your belt to dictate the size and style of buckle you choose. A 3-inch-wide buckle on a 3/4-inch belt doesn't present a good picture. Straight western

belts are normally 1 1/2 inches wide, and tapered belts are usually 1 1/4 inches at the back, tapering to 3/4 or 1 inch at the buckle area. Women and kids often like a 1 1/4-inch belt for less bulk at the waist.

Sterling silver overlay is more expensive than German silver or a manufacturer's brand-name alloy, and hand engraving, contrasting precious metals, and other custom flourishes can add hundreds of dollars to the price of a buckle. Not all show organizations require a belt, so if you're wearing a blazer, vest, or jacket that completely covers your waistline, consider dispensing with the belt altogether for a trimmer look.

- **Conchos:** These circles of silver can be sterling or German silver and are frequently decorated with overlaid gold work and fastened to the saddle, the bridle, the bit, and/or a cowboy's spurs and sometimes his chaps.

In the show pen, you can ride without accessories, but you can't show off without them! While showmen just select a nice scarf and they're ready to show, today's accessories are the small finishing touches that capture a woman's personality and make her western show outfit look different from any other. Earrings, hair accessories, pins and pendants, ties, number pins, spurs, and other small accents add interest to your presentation. And while these baubles aren't usually required to show, they're fun to collect and fun to wear, and will add to the feeling of confidence you want to experience by being impeccably turned out when you step into the show ring.

Jewelry

Today's riders often dress up their hatbands with sterling buckles and gemstone accents. If your hat has a nice factory-installed band, it's probably best to leave it. Aftermarket bands should be considered only if they really add something special to your outfit, but think subtle: feathers and rhinestones probably look better on the dance floor than in the show arena. Hat pins and stampede strings are also best left in the trailer if you're a part of the walk-jog-lope crowd.

Earrings can create a frame for a woman's face, and should tie in with your outfit, adding to the overall theme. Wearing leather and rhinestones? Think fancy, glitzy earrings. Sporting a southwestern tapestry vest? Look for silver earrings with a geometric pattern that echo a design in your vest. Not sure what ear decor is best? Then opt for classic silver conchos, about an inch in diameter or smaller, to go perfectly with any western outfit. Dangling or jiggly earrings are a bad idea. They are distracting and can make your horse appear bouncy. They can also make your ears sore after a long day in the saddle.

V-neck or scoop-neck vests and jackets are the perfect place to put a piece of jewelry or a tie at the neck to complete the look. If you like to wear traditional blouses with collars, consider a pretty brooch that matches your earrings, or wear a pretied scarf with a closure that's hidden under the collar roll.

For slinky tops, think of pendants, pins, and beautiful chains that lie in place yet fill the neckline and add interest as the judge looks toward your face. Be sure the size and style of the jewelry complement the rest of your outfit, and also check that your accent piece stays in place as you ride. Pendants with pin backs can be worn with or without a chain, and won't slide around if you use the pin backing to anchor the ornament to your slinky top's front.

Speaking of jewelry, don't forget number pins. Whether you show with your identification number on your back or on your saddle blanket, there are numerous clever ornaments on the market that will attach that number and look much nicer than safety pins. Remember, little things add up to a lot, and if you want to make a great presentation, don't overlook even the smallest detail. Worried about holes in leather garments? Either pin your number to your blanket, or use number pins in the same holes in your garment every time. Show tip: Put your number on your garment before you put the garment on.

Scarves

For a jaunty Ascot look, try a regular scarf (about 20 inches square) rolled and knotted at the neck, with the knot in front and tails tied under the collar in back. A small scarf can be worn bandito style, triangle pointing down, with a pretty pin anchoring it in the center. Rosette ties and ties made from ultrasuede to match your chaps can be useful to have in the tie collection as well, depending on your taste and blouse assortment.

While slinky tops are the most popular look today to wear with vests and jackets, remember that their thin knit necklines won't support a scarf or a tie of any kind.

Treasure Hunting

Western stores and tack catalogs are the place to search for interesting, unique accessories, but don't overlook antiques malls, flea markets, and even thrift shops for interesting vintage pieces to give a one-of-a-kind touch to your outfit.

Gloves

Cowboys use gloves to protect their hands. Today, in most associations, wearing gloves is a matter of personal preference. If you wear them during practice you'll be more comfortable manipulating your reins in the show pen with gloves. In general, gloves are worn in events where the human, not the horse, is being judged: showmanship and horsemanship primarily. If you are going to use them, match your glove color to either your sleeve or your chap color, and if you can't find a great match, go darker rather than lighter. You can sometimes get a good match dying nylon gloves at home, but they are slippery to ride in and you may lose your mind trying to get the right shade. Also, gloves that are long enough to tuck up under your sleeves are better for riding than what are usually promoted as show gloves, which are often so short they peel back and show a strip of your wrist. You can minimize that possibility by using black or appropriately colored electrical tape to snug the glove openings around your forearm, under your sleeves. Always have an extra pair of gloves in your trailer or tack box: like socks, gloves have a solitary nature and tend to get separated from their mates.

The Story of the Cowboy Hat
(Written by Bret and Linda of the Priest Hat Company)

The cowboy hat is an icon that is recognized worldwide. No other one piece of gear or apparel expresses more about traditional American culture than the "cowboy hat." It is an instantly recognizable statement of our heritage and history, which speaks to all who view it, of the independence and romance of the untamed west.

In the nineteenth century hats were an essential part of a man's wardrobe. In the late 1800s a good hat could easily cost a man a month's wages. The most common style of western hats of the time came with a flat brim and an open crown. The buyer would crease it to the desired shape. It was possible to tell where a person was from by the crease in his hat. If a man was from a damp, snowy climate he wouldn't want the moisture to gather in the crown. If he was from a drier climate, the crease didn't matter as much. Some folks even came up with a family crease that would set them apart from their neighbors.

When the West opened up to the cattle business after the Civil War, photographic records show cowboys wearing top hats or bowlers. The shorter brims on these hats didn't offer much protection from the elements. Enter John B. Stetson of Philadelphia. The son of a hat maker, Stetson began building hats with wider brims in the 1860s. He called his new hat "The Boss of the Plains," and it was an instant hit. Stetson's "Boss of the Plains" is credited as being the first "cowboy" hat, but long before Stetson came along, the Vaqueros of Mexico and California wore hats that had a flat brim and a flat open crown, similar in style to Stetson's "Boss of the Plains." Today, Priest Hat Company builds quite a few hats based on the Vaquero hat, which is a very popular style with customers, especially in California, Nevada, Idaho, and Oregon, among working cowboys (a Priest hat modeled on the Vaquero hat of old appears on the cover of this book).

In the 1840s, a device called the Conformator (shown in the photo on this page) was invented in Paris, France.

With this piece of equipment, a hatter could produce a scale pattern of a customer's head, which then allowed the hatter to make a hat to an exact shape and size. Mercantile stores that sold factory-built hats also used the device to shape their stock hats to their customer's heads.

Today, we have several of the old conformators in our shop and thousands of patterns from years gone by.

The measuring device known as a Conformator.

Hats today are built much the same way they were 150 years ago. Factory-made hats are built using modern automated equipment. There are only about sixty custom hat companies left in the United States. Most of these hatters produce their hats by hand, using antique equipment. Tools of the trade are hard to find and the knowledge of how to build a quality hat is even more elusive.

I am frequently asked how I got into the hat-making business. The answer is that for many years I was constantly frustrated when I went into a western store to buy a hat. The hats they carried looked like they were made by a cookie cutter. I would buy one, then end up remodeling it.

I worked on my own hats, cleaning and creasing for a number of years before I discovered custom hats. There was a small hat shop in Eagle, Idaho, the Priest Hat Company, which could build any kind of hat imaginable. I applied for a job and was hired. Having been a carpenter, I was used to working with my hands and quickly picked up on my new trade with gusto. I found the challenge of taking a raw piece of felt and turning it into a fine hat extremely gratifying.

Priest Hat Company was started by Randy Priest in the 1970s. Randy learned his trade under Manetta Shrite. Manetta continued to make hats into her late 80s. In 2005 she passed away at the age of 96. After I began to master my new vocation, the owner of the company offered to sell me the business. My wife, Linda, and I had been planning a move to Montana, where we eventually wanted to start our own hat business in the Flathead Valley, but after some debate we decided to take the plunge and purchased the Priest Hat Company.

Historically, hatters have been very secretive about their trade. To this day the same is true. Many of the processes in making quality hats are guarded trade secrets that are handed down from generation to generation.

One of the first hats I built for myself is known as a Packer (see the photo on the following page). It was the hat I had been looking for in the western stores but could not find. A Packer is designed to be used in the high country. It is compact and does well in wet locations. As you can see from the photo, my packer hat has seen a lot of use. After many years of wear, a hat will develop a patina and a character of its own. I always tell people that every well-used hat tells a story.

About seven years ago I had some folks bring a hat to me for renovation (as shown in the photo on the following page). The hat was very old, but it was still in pretty good shape. When I asked the history of the hat, they reported they had inherited it from a man who had passed away a few years back. He had worn the hat at the Pendleton Roundup in the

The Packer.

1920s when he won All-Around Cowboy in the rodeo. His hat was a prized possession and was one of the few things he owned at the time of his death. I recommended they clean and restore the hat with its original components, but not renovate it. After I had finished working on the old hat I took photos of it, and noted the dimensions of the crown, brim, and so on. In honor of the cowboy who once owned the hat, I built one just like it and call it the Pendleton.

Some other common questions I get are:

- What is a good hat made from?

- How do you make a hat?

- How long does it take to make a hat?

The finest hats are made from beaver fur. Belly fur is the best. Often the fur is blended with European hare fur and sometimes nutria fur. Most of the hats that we build are a blend because a blend produces the most consistent bodies (a body is the raw felt in the rough form of a hat). To build a hat we start by going over the customer's order to determine

The Pendleton.

the proper dimensions and size of the hat. We then chose a correctly sized block for the desired style. The body is then steamed and stretched over the block, sizing it and setting the height of the crown. Following this, the crown is ironed with an antique device called a crown iron, which sets the shape of the open crown. After the felt has cooled and cured for some time, the crown is then pounced. This process finishes the felt: the finer the finish the better the hat. If a hat is not properly finished it will tend to wick water and not hold up in the elements.

Now the block is removed and the crown is fitted over a form of the customer's head. This stage of the process assures the wearer of a proper fit. After the crown and brim are formed the body is dried. The brim is then heated and pressed with a plating machine two different times under approximately 40,000 pounds. The brim is then pounced to a fine finish. The hat is now ready for all the trimmings such as the sweatband (we choose to sew our sweatbands in by hand), grosgrain ribbon, bound brim, liner, and sometimes a stampede string. To shape the hat we steam it and crease it by hand. The creasing can be compared to sculpting. Each hat is built one at a time much like an original piece of art. When the hat is finished we allow it to dry out completely. The hat is then carefully packaged into a heavy-duty hatbox and shipped to the customer. It takes three to four days from start to finish to build most custom hats.

If you're interested in studying this dying art form or becoming a hatter and starting a business of your own, we offer a hatter's apprenticeship (call 208-278-3227). The course is broken into several one-week modules and while you may never want to build a hat for someone else, we can guarantee there is no satisfaction like building your own hat, which is a living piece of the history of the Old West.

Chapter 6

Winning Western Horsemanship

with Nancy Cahill

Getting Your Horse Physically and Mentally Ready

Western horsemanship is a class that puts horses and riders through a pattern consisting of various maneuvers in order to evaluate the skills of both the horse and the rider. The horse should accept every command from the rider without resistance and move from one transition to the next, executing each maneuver in a relaxed frame, with his head and neck level with the withers. The rider should maintain correct body position while delivering subtle cues to the horse. Every move should say that the pair is a team, working together.

The judge is looking for the rider who has the ability to move a horse through the western horsemanship pattern with good form. The horse's movement is not judged; rather the ability of the rider to make the horse move at his best is considered. For example, if the rider allows the horse to four beat at the lope with no intervention, that would be penalized. The judge is responsible for posting a pattern in advance so that the riders will have time to study it. It is the responsibility of the entrant to know the pattern and if necessary ask the judge for clarification. A judge may have each rider come in from the gate or may bring all entries in and have them line up on the rail. If riders come in one at a time, there should be a working order to be in line and ready to ride. After each rider has performed the pattern individually, they may be asked to line up at the opposite end or leave the arena and wait for their number to be called back for rail work. The rail work is usually a tiebreaker for pattern work, but all placings can change if the entry performs poorly on the rail after a nice pattern. Rail work should consist of all three gaits—walk, trot, and lope in at least one direction of the arena. When working on the rail, the exhibitor should pay attention to the position of their horse as well as the other exhibitor's horses. If horses are asked to reverse, they should always reverse to the inside of the arena. Each horse should have a number pinned on either side of the saddle pad that is easily visible to the judge.

Pattern Work

Pattern work may consist of many combinations of maneuvers. A horse and rider may be asked to perform the following gaits: walk, trot, extended trot, lope, extended lope in circles, straight lines, serpentines, curved lines, figure-8s, or any combination of these. Turns on the haunches, turns on the forehand, spins, rollbacks, lead changes both simple or flying—these are just a sampling of actions that may be required. Riding with no stirrups, two tracking, side passing, and backing are all acceptable. When a judge draws a pattern, he or she takes into consideration the level of rider. If it is a novice class, the pattern should consist of maneuvers that are expected of beginner riders. The judge would not ask for complicated lead changes and spins, for instance, in classes of this level. When drawing the pattern for advanced riders, the judge may use any combination of difficult maneuvers to separate those who possess more skill and knowledge.

A Winning Ride

A winning ride in the western horsemanship division has its beginning long before you and your horse enter the arena. In fact, the journey begins before you even put your foot in the stirrup. A winning ride begins with careful study of the horse; his conformation, breeding, health, attitude, and physical needs, and his talent and abilities. The horse and rider should move smoothly through all transitions of gait and direction and have the look of a confident team.

Wanted: Rider with Detective Skills

If you have not bred and raised the horse you are using, you need to find out all you can about the horse's history. Knowing what has taken place in a horse's life before you acquired him may offer clues to strange or undesirable behavior. An example of this is the case of a mare I was riding at a show. When management turned on the overhead fans, she left so hard she nearly hurt herself and everyone else in the ring. At the time I wanted to get mad at her, but I gave her the benefit of the doubt, and just did my best to get her under control.

Later, I did some belated research by calling the previous owner. What I found out gave me the explanation for the mare's bizarre reaction to the fans. Her previous owner told me the mare had been the only survivor in a tornado that blew away the entire barn she was in; only the stall around her was left standing. When a horse has had a serious negative experience, especially if he has been mishandled or mistreated at the hands of humans, he measures all human beings by what he knows and what he knows is forever shaped by that particular experience. It can take a long time to regain the confidence of an abused or injured horse and some may never trust again. But at least by knowing the history of your horse, you will be better equipped to foresee issues that might arise in the future.

Before mounting the horse, a savvy competitor will make every effort to know their horse as well their own child. If the horse has been in their possession their entire life, this is an easy task. Knowing the answers to certain questions—such as whether he eats well everyday; whether he is always a fresh horse no matter how hot or cold the weather; or whether he has any maintenance issues—doesn't just give you an edge in the show ring, it also decreases risk factors for both rider and horse.

Care of Your Horse

Horses rely on people for their well-being; so good *horsemanship* includes making sure that the horse is capable of performing the task that is being asked of him. Whoever said, "No hoof, no horse!" was making the truest of statements. A horse who is not sound cannot perform. It is necessary to take good care of a horse's hooves through good nutrition as well as with a good farrier. Can you imagine yourself trying to run a marathon with blisters on your feet? Good veterinary care is also critical for the equine athlete. Health care includes an excellent deworming program, good nutrition (which can be a huge factor in a horse's health, and consequently his performance capabilities), dental work (since we ride most of the time with a bit in the horse's mouth, if it is uncomfortable for whatever reason, it can easily lead to a behavior problem), and a vaccination schedule (to ensure the horse is protected against contagious diseases).

Mares

Mares come with their own special issues. Dealing with a mare in heat can require some special handling tactics. You need to know if your mare's attitude and/or behavior changes when she is in season, since this could well impact her performance in the show ring. If she turns from Dr. Jekyl into Ms. Hyde when she's in season, a vet may need to

---

It's the Little Things

Did you know:

- Weather can be a factor in your deworming program. If you live in a very cold climate, there will be enough of a freeze to kill many parasites and you won't have to deworm as often as you would if you live in a warm climate. In the North, deworming four times a year may be sufficient, but in Texas, we deworm every six to eight weeks. Wormers are rotated throughout the year so parasites cannot build up a systemic resistance.

- Different vaccines are needed in different parts of the country, so not only must you know what vaccines are required for your area, but you must also be aware of what your horse may exposed to when you take him to a show outside of his local environment. You should know how many doses of a vaccine are necessary, as well as the time it takes for the vaccine to provide your horse with full immunity.

check her reproductive tract for abnormalities. Controlling a mare's cycling abilities has come a long way in the last few years. Depending on the show schedule, a mare may be put on progesterone products to keep her from cycling, which makes it possible to show her under more normal circumstances.

Is Your Horse Right for Western Horsemanship?

Now that you are sure your horse is physically and mentally ready to ride, let's see whether he is the right horse for the job. In this case, we are considering a horse for western horsemanship classes. Good horsemanship begins before you enter the ring and takes many hours of dedicated work and sharpening of skills for both horse and rider. The journey to the winner's circle can be made easier if you select a horse whose disposition allows him to adapt to the requirements of the class. A good horsemanship horse must stand patiently, move in large or small increments of distance, transition from fast to slow and vice versa, and stop and back on command. This doesn't sound much different from what is asked of horses in other disciplines, but the finesse that is required to win in a western horsemanship class is what makes the difference.

A high-strung horse *may* become a good horsemanship horse, but it can take many years of work to teach him the patience and exactness that is needed for a winning performance. A part of being a good competitor in this class. then, is the ability to analyze this aspect about your horse and act upon what you know. If you realize your horse is the type who wants to move fast, cover ground, and is constantly "busy," and you don't want to get a different horse, you've got a tough decision. You can continue toward your horsemanship goals knowing that your success may be limited and that arriving at the desired results will definitely require a great deal of patience on your part. Or you can adjust your competitive goals by focusing your efforts on a division that better suits your horse's type and personality. The point is that every horse must be evaluated, not just before you purchase him, but also periodically during training, by asking, "Is he working out in this job and does he enjoy it?"

Maintaining Control

One word defines what good horsemanship is all about: control. The horse must allow the rider to totally dictate his every move. Control is easy to say and so hard to achieve. Let's think about a horse's basic nature. They tend to think that they were put on the earth to move from one blade of grass to another. When they are expected to perform all of the skills that we ask of them, they probably wonder why. Our only way to communicate that answer is through our actions and aids. Since we cannot vocally speak their language, we have to rely on a series of repetitive actions. How do we go about this? As riders, our hands, legs, seat, weight, voice, and most of all our brain are used to communicate our thoughts to the horse. These same "aids" are needed in achieving good horsemanship.

Good Control Comes from a Correct Rider Position

Basic riding position has the rider sitting centered on the horse. Since the body is positioned with one leg draped on either side of the horse, balance is achieved through symmetry. Accepted body position has a vertical line drawn through the ear, shoulder, hip, and heel (as shown in the photos on this page and the next) in the English disciplines and does not differ much when sitting in a western saddle.

In western horsemanship, the reins are held in one hand, a little to one side of the saddle horn, with a slight bend in the elbow. The free

A western rider seen from the side showing correct posture and alignment.

Darrell Dodds Photography

(Left) The tension in this rider's body will allow for very little feel of her horse or timing in the delivery of her aids. (Right) Here we see a rider who exhibits the tall yet relaxed posture necessary to execute the required patterns fluidly, with grace and good timing.

hand is held in a similar position, mirroring the hand that is holding the reins. Your chin is up so your eyes are looking in the direction you are going. Your shoulders should be square without being "stiff," and the back is straight. Stirrups should be adjusted to allow a slight, comfortable bend in your knee while allowing you to carry your with heels down. Form to function always applies in good horsemanship. When the rider is sitting in a position that complements the horse's movement, the cues that are given become invisible. Invisible cues are the height of good horsemanship. That oneness between horse and rider is what makes a winning combination.

The Role Your Hands Play in Controlling Your Horse

Your hands communicate direction and control the horse from the shoulders forward. They must be slow and fluid because a horse cannot see the speed and direction of the hands until he feels the pressure on the

Darrell Dodds Photograph

In this photo we see an example of a rider whose reins are much too long, causing her hands to move up and out of position. With her reins carried in this manner, this rider cannot possibly give the subtle bridle aids demanded in a winning western horsemanship performance.

neck and from the bit. Your hands should be carried low and relaxed. With a bend in your elbow, the forearm of your rein hand should form a straight line to your horse's mouth. The reins should be held with light contact on the horse's mouth. During training, the rider must give the horse time to process the information that has been given. It may start with a firm cue that over time is reduced to an invisible one. For instance, you may have to use two hands for many months to ask your horse to give his nose to the left and right. Eventually, the horse comes to know and understand what you expect from him when you apply a specific cue and it takes less and less information for the horse to "get it" and execute the action(s) you desire. Soon just one hand and a light touch mean the same thing as two hands did many months before. All of this is repeated over and over again until the horse and rider are a team.

Darrell Dodds Photograph

Here we see the same rider with her rein length correctly adjusted to allow her to communicate with her horse through subtle movements of her fingers, wrists, and hands.

The Role of Your Legs

Legs control impulsion and direction. Your legs also help stabilize your seat. Heels should be lower than the toes, with the lower leg under the knee. The ball of the foot should be in the center of the stirrup. Imagine how you would want to stay centered if you were walking between two electric wires. Now imagine trying to stay centered in that same way as you sit in your saddle. Your legs and bridle reins act like those "hot wires" for the horse. You must keep his body between those "wires" in order to have total control. Your legs give the horse the information of what speed is desired as well as which direction is intended. Getting your horse to move easily and fluidly away from your leg pressure is one of the many skills that must be mastered in good horsemanship. This is called lateral control and allows you to get the maneuver called the side-pass from your horse. By applying varying pressures with your legs, you give your horse information on the speed you desire. Depending on your horse's sensitivity, it could just be a touch of your calf, or it might necessitate a spur. Knowing your horse will prepare you to know what to expect from him in response time, and that information will help you decide how best to cue him during competition. Too much pressure will make him appear high strung and overreactive. Too little pressure may leave you with a sluggish response or no response at all. Solving those issues are a part of what you will do with your horse during your training time between competitions.

By sitting in the center of the horse, your weight is distributed equally across the horse's back. Just by moving slightly to one side or the other, you can then manipulate the horse's balance to make him move left or right. This can be used to a rider's advantage. On the other hand, if you aren't centered on your horse, your position can *hinder* his performance.

Don't Forget Your Voice

The voice is an important part of good horsemanship. When all mechanical cues that are visible to the eye are eliminated, the voice is part of delivering the invisible cue. Whoa is a universal word for the stop. When the rein hand is not raised, the horse appears to be stopping without any information from the rider. By using a word to descend from lope to trot or walk, transitions become effortless. Using the same word repetitively gives the horse a sound that he can associate with the maneuver that he is being asked to perform.

The Most Important Tool for Controlling Your Horse: Your Brain

Most important of all is your brain. If you are not smarter than the horse, you have already lost the battle. You must learn to think like a horse. This comes over time, not overnight. Horses are just like people in that they are all individuals. What works on one might not work on the next one. Safety is the biggest issue for rider and horse, so losing your temper will get you nowhere. Before you get into a heated battle think through situations and ask yourself why the horse might be doing something. If you allow your interaction with your horse to deteriorate into

A Softly Spoken Word

The tone of a rider's voice can easily turn a nervous horse into a quiet and trusting one. It matters little what you say; more important is how you say it.

force, more often than not you will lose, either in lost time or in injury to you or the horse. Riders must remember that they were in school for many years to learn what they know, so it will also take a horse a long time to achieve every skill they need to know.

Outfitting Yourself and Your Horse

Aids are the tools of anyone who chooses to ride. Becoming a good rider allows you to optimize your natural aids. Then there is the equipment you use. Western saddles come in many shapes, sizes, and colors. The most important consideration is that the saddle fits the horse and the rider. More often than not, an ill-fitting saddle will cause a behavior problem. You couldn't do your job if the equipment you wore made you sore. Saddles should be clean and show that the rider cares about his gear. Nowadays, the saddles used in western horsemanship are adorned with silver and intricate carving. Don't let this confuse the issue. This event is still about the ability of the rider to communicate with the horse using the proper form. Headstalls may be silver laden and should fit the horse. A bulky headstall will not complement a very petite-headed horse. Silver adornment should never be a factor in judging. Tack that is clean and well-oiled shows that the rider cares.

Clothing can range from extremely fancy, as well as costly, to a clean starched shirt. This is entirely up to the individual. The American Quarter Horse Association rulebook states that a participant must wear long pants, a long-sleeved shirt with collar, cowboy boots, and a western hat. That leaves a great deal of room for individuality. Spurs and chaps are optional.

When choosing a bit for showing, consideration should be given to the horse's training. You'll also need to check the rulebook to see which bits are legal in your division or class, and from those options, pick the one that gives you ultimate control and makes your horse content. It may take several tries to find the one that works best, but don't get caught in the trap of thinking that a different bit will solve any problem. Most performance problems that come up need to be corrected with *training*, not a bit change.

Selection of tack and clothing should be designed to complement the rider's horsemanship abilities. The last thing a rider wants to do is to draw the judge's eye to a weakness. A competitor needs to look the part of a professional horseman or horsewoman, with a tasteful presentation.

How the Class Is Judged

The western horsemanship class is judged on a point system. Points are allocated from 0 to 20. Ten points are dedicated to evaluating the appearance of both horse and rider and the position of the rider. A perfect pattern and rail work are not all that is considered. A judge has the right to penalize the exhibitor if the horse is too thin, lethargic, dull, or overly tired. An overly stiff and artificial rider who has the appearance of just riding the saddle and not the horse will also be penalized. Faults are measured on the severity and frequency of the infractions. Some minor faults on the rider's part are looking down, incorrect rein length, sloppy position, dirty tack, or staring at the judge. Performance faults might include crooked backing, failure to hold a pivot foot on a turn, oblong circles, or break of gait for a few strides. Severe faults resulting in low scores are touching the horse, omission of a maneuver, knocking over a cone, severe disobedience, or kicking. These faults will not disqualify an exhibitor, but they will prevent that rider from placing over any other exhibitor who performs the pattern correctly. Causes for disqualification include abuse, a fall by horse or rider, illegal equipment, wearing the wrong number, or a horse consistently carrying his head and neck too low.

By knowing the class procedures before going in, riders should know what is expected from their performance. Knowing the rules prevents costly mistakes that could have been remedied from the start. Now that you know what is expected, how do you go about making that perfect western horsemanship run? First, be honest with yourself about your abilities and experiences. There is no room for a big ego when you are learning to be the best you can be. If you continually find yourself left out of the ribbons, don't just assume the judge held a prejudiced opinion. Check your own opinion of your riding ability with a friend or a professional coach or trainer. Another pair of eyes can often see what you may not feel. Feel is one of the most important components of riding and only comes from hours and hours of time spent on and around horses. The more horses you are able to experience—the good as well as the bad—the more you learn about feel. With feel comes timing, which is the ingredient necessary to polish your ability to answer all the questions found in a horsemanship pattern: what, where, when, and how. What maneuver will you ask the horse to perform? Where will you ask him to perform it? When must you set up your horse for the maneuver in order to allow him time to successfully execute it well. And how

Troubleshooting Tips for Competition Day

Keep the following tips in mind:

- Don't watch another rider doing fabulous spins and then decide that your horse should do those fast spins also. Your horse may not be at that level yet and he'll only be afraid when asked to do more than he is capable of doing. Ride what you brought with you. There is no reason that you can't work to that level, but in due time.

- When practicing at home, ride with the proper form at all times. If you wait until you get to the show ring to change your position in the saddle and/or the way you give your signals, your horse may not recognize you as the one he is comfortable with at home.

- Learn the pattern through and through. Walk it unmounted, then practice each maneuver on your horse separately once or twice in the warm-up arena so you have all the parts down pat.

- Once in the arena, mentally talk yourself through each part of the pattern.

- Have a positive attitude; the look on your face will tell the tale to a judge.

- You paid for the judges' time, so don't be apologetic for being there. Work to do your best, but remember to enjoy your time in the spotlight.

- Ride your horse through his weak spots and capitalize on his virtues. You can never be sure a fellow competitor won't have the same problems.

- Dress to impress. Dark colors are good if you are short or heavy. Light colors will emphasize any unwanted motion in your body position or legs.

- Practice patience. It may take many runs to gain consistency in western horsemanship.

- Show against yourself first and strive for perfection before you try riding to beat other competitors.

A positive mental attitude plays a big part in a rider's success.

should you go about asking him to do it (aids sequence, pressure levels, and so on)? All these questions will have to be answered every time you ask a horse for any gait, transition, turn, or the like. Since horses also have a brain, riding is like no other sport. You can't just put them in a closet to be used when you find it convenient.

What makes the horsemanship class such a challenge is that while these or similar questions are asked and answered by riders and their horses every day in the normal process of riding, in a horsemanship class all these questions will come to pass in the span of a minute. The horse must be taught all of the fundamental basics of riding before he can be asked to combine difficult maneuvers. While basics involve the horse going forward, backward, left, and right, putting them together is what gets the team through a horsemanship class.

When practicing at home, set the cones used as markers for the pattern in various configurations. By inventing new directions and making transitions, the rider can determine the weak points in his horse or his own skills, and work to improve them. Resist the temptation to ride the same pattern over and over. Horses tend to memorize patterns and will anticipate each move. This will show up in the show ring as well. A good approach is to separate the maneuvers during schooling, make sure your horse executes each one correctly, then blend them together smoothly in a finished "pattern." Once you think you have it together at home, it's time to try it in the show ring.

Pattern Strategy

Homework won't help you if you walk into the arena and have no strategy for performing the pattern. How tight does the judge have the pattern set? Where is the judge sitting in relation to the pattern? Are the cones close to the fence? Are you going to enter one at a time or all at once? These questions demand quick assessments before you walk up to the first marker.

For most patterns, you will begin at the first marker and go either to the left or the right of the cones. If it is not necessary to stand close to the marker, give yourself room by standing 10 or 12 feet to the side. That way if the horse steps too far left or right when he departs, there will be room for correction. Standing too close gives no room for error and you stand the chance of knocking the marker over. How close should the horse stand in relation to entering the pattern? The judge is more interested in you being ready to perform than he is in having the horse's front feet on the line where the pattern begins. If the horse's hooves are within 6 or 8 feet, then you are showing your intent to begin the pattern as soon as the judge signals. Look at the judge and stand still when you are waiting at the marker. It is too late to adjust your position or correct your horse's headset. Doing so will relate to the judge that you are not pre-pared, nor are you confident.

As you enter the pattern at the prescribed gait, do so with smoothness and ease (see the diagram on the following page). You want the pattern to blend together with no glaring errors. Even the best of intentions go awry sometimes, so if your pattern begins to unravel try to keep yourself and your horse together and make the best of it. A good save is good horsemanship. Your horse may have spooked at the judge and taken the wrong lead. Knowing it and correcting it shows the judge that you can fix a problem. If you have the ability to cover up an error, and make the judge believe that nothing went amiss, that's good horsemanship. Just because you know that there was a mistake, it doesn't always mean that the judge or spectators knew it as well. Keep riding no matter what may happen. When completing the pattern, make sure that you don't exit the arena or move to the rail in the path of the next exhibitor's pattern. That is poor sportsmanship even if it was an accident.

While waiting for the other competitors to complete their patterns, you should sit quietly at the other end of the arena or on the rail, so as not to distract the horse who is on course. If you were excused from the arena one at a time, listen outside for the possibility of your number being among the callbacks. If you are called back to the finals, enter the arena at the prescribed gait and leave plenty of room between your horse and the one entering in front of you. Keep a positive look on your face to go with your good posture and light hands. A judge may not use your horse that day, but they do remember good showmanship and a good atti-tude. Make the judge want to use you.

Part of good horsemanship is being proud of what you have accom-plished. None of us ever think that there isn't something we might have done better—that is simply striving to be your best. But remember also to give yourself a pat on the back for every achievement, no matter how small it might seem. Every competitor should congratulate the winners and humbly accept those same congratulations. There is something to be learned every time you and your horse enter the arena. Hard work, rep-etition, desire, consistency, and a great attitude are what separate the wannabes from the champions.

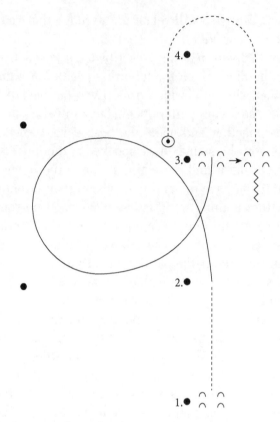

A strategy for performing a pattern.

Performing the Pattern

You have been given the pattern, now you will study it until you can recite it word for word. After practicing the different parts and maybe putting it together once or twice in the warm-up arena, it's time for the class.

- **Marker 1** (*directions: at marker 1, jog*): You should not approach it too closely until the exhibitor on course is near the end of their pattern. Sit quietly so your horse will not become nervous. Horses know when the time has come, and if you are tense your horse will be, too. When the judge signals that it is your turn, cue the horse softly for the trot. If you kick or give a voice command that is too forceful, the horse could read it as a lope off. As the pattern begins, the rider should be thinking as well as looking toward the next transition, the lope departure.

- **Marker 2** (*lope left lead, circle left*): Each horse will be different as to how much leg it will take to make the lope departure. If he is a little lazy, the rider needs to cue him slightly earlier than the rider with a sensitive horse. The horse should be loping at the marker. The rider should have his head turned slightly left, looking ahead around the circle. The circle should be the largest one the rider can draw and still stay within the markers. This will look much smoother than a tiny one. A small one will make it more difficult to get to the next transition. When you close the circle your eyes should be on marker 3 and the spot where you will stop, not looking down at your horse.

- **Marker 3** (*Stop, sidepass right two horses' widths, back five steps*): Bring your horse to a smooth stop, with the marker positioned somewhere between his shoulder and your leg. Stopping short of the marker will make it appear that you were in a hurry to stop, and stopping beyond it will make it look as though your horse wasn't obedient. Settle your horse briefly before you perform the right sidepass. This should blend together and be very smooth. Nothing looks worse than a crooked sidepass, so keep the horse perpendicular to the end of the arena. Only go as far as the pattern designated. It does not look better to go further right just because the horse is not moving smoothly. Your eyes should be up and looking forward the whole time. After completing the sidepass, balance and settle your horse before asking him to back up. Back straight five steps. If your horse begins to drift to one side while backing, you hand and legs should straighten him immediately and invisibly. Each of the five steps is counted when each of your horse's front legs moves backward. Hesitate to show the judge that you've finished the maneuver.

- **Marker 4** (*extend trot around marker 4*): You will cue your horse for the trot, before adding the speed of the extension. If the rider asks too quickly, the likelihood of a lope departure is high. A voice-commanded trot may make it possible to use less leg. The horse will not be confused with the two commands. A cluck or a kissing noise will be enough for the horse to distinguish between the two maneuvers. After two or three trotting steps, move your horse into the extension. This will make the maneuver blend and will also safeguard against a break of gait. When trotting around marker 4, sit very still since the angle could push the horse into a lope. There is also a loss of momentum around the marker, so the rider may have to push after making the turn to keep the extension uniform.

- **Return to Marker 3** (*stop straight at marker, execute a 360-degree turn left*): Don't ask your horse to turn faster than is comfortable. A forced turn looks as though the rider's hand is going faster than the horse's feet. Be sure to start and end the turn at the same point. If the horse stops at 350 and is short of the starting point, it leaves a bad last impression on a judge, so don't be in a rush to complete your pattern and leave. When you complete the pattern, acknowledge the judge and proceed to the rail or out of the arena.

A Look at Western Pleasure

Western pleasure has long been an entry-level class for horses and riders. The basic gaits for any western horse are walk, jog, and lope. The manner in which the horse performs these gaits is the criteria for judging this event. A good pleasure horse takes free-flowing strides that match his size and conformation. A horse who is 14.1 hands (small) can take a much smaller stride than one who is 16.1 hands (8 inches taller). Most pleasure horses are of medium height and conformation. They are built like a ballet dancer who moves with style and grace. When each hoof strikes the ground, it should do so lightly and effortlessly and cover the amount of ground in keeping with the horse's conformation.

Movement and Manners

Movement and manners are the basis for western pleasure. The good pleasure horse should look like the one that everyone would like to take home and ride. The head and neck should be held in a relaxed position, but not lower than the withers (as shown in the photo on this page).

Keep your horse's head and neck in a relaxed position.

This position allows the horse to carry himself up in the shoulders and be very collected. The horse's head should be in a natural, relaxed position, but not behind the vertical. There should be no look of intimidation, and the horse's ears should be alert. The reins should be loose, but the horse should be under control at all times. All transitions should be smooth and immediate when called for. All gaits should be cadenced and balanced.

Most stock horse breeds have several age groups for horses and skill levels for the riders. Junior horses are considered 5 years old and under and senior horses are 6 years old and over. Junior horses are allowed to be shown with two hands as they are learning and need more help than a senior horse. They are shown in a snaffle bit or a hackamore with two hands. If a curb bit is used, the rider must use only one hand on the reins. Senior horses are to be shown in a curb bridle with one hand. If the horse is shown with two hands, the reins must be crossed over the neck and held near the pommel and have about 8 inches between hands. Two-year-old horses are allowed to be shown after July 1 of the year of their second birthday.

Riders are also divided into groups according to age and skill. There is novice western pleasure for riders who are new to the event. This gives them the chance to ride with people who have the same skill level as they do. There are also age divisions for youth riders, who are usually divided into 13 years old and under, and 14 to 18 years old. Amateur classes are offered to those over 18 years old who do not ride professionally. Open classes are for anyone who wants to show and are usually dominated by professionals. Professionals cannot show in any class except the open.

Class Protocol

Horses enter the arena at a walk or a jog on the rail. The smart rider tries to position the horse so the judge will have an unobstructed view of the horse at every gait. If one horse travels faster or with a bigger stride, the horse is allowed to pass on the inside. It is unwise, however, to continue to ride off the rail, because continually lapping the other riders may cause your horse to appear as though he is traveling too fast. There is no penalty for passing as long as your horse maintains his collection and rhythm. After passing, be sure to return to the rail smoothly and in a manner that doesn't cut off horses coming up behind you.

The size of the arena dictates the number of horses who may go to the rail at one time. There needs to be enough room for all entries to show their horses without crowding. Usually in an arena of average size, fifteen horses would be the appropriate number to go on the rail. A maximum of twelve horses are allowed if the extended lope is called for. It is possible for many entries to be in a pleasure class. When this is the case, there may be splits. For instance, if there were thirty in the class, the arena would not hold that many horses. The judge would split the horses into two heats of fifteen each. Each heat would work separately and the judge would pick seven or eight from each heat to come back for a working final. The horses would then work the rail again.

A backup is a requirement and would be asked for either on the rail or in the center of the arena. A good, light, immediate backup is part of the judging process. After satisfying all class criteria, the judge places the class from first to tenth if there are ten or more in the class.

Horses are asked to perform both directions of the arena. The judge will make all calls for gait changes and may reverse the horses at any time. All gaits must be demonstrated in both directions and an extension of gaits is called for in a least one direction. During an extended trot, you should show actual lengthening of your horse's stride, not just speed. This is true at the lope as well. All transitions should be smooth and look effortless. When reversing, horses must turn toward the center of the arena at the walk or trot only.

The walk is a four-beat gait, as each hoof moves independently of the next. Try to keep your horse's walk active. While it should appear comfortable to ride, it should also cover ground. The jog is a two-beat gait that has the diagonal pairs of legs moving in unison. The primary difference between an English trot and a western jog is not how the horse moves his legs, but rather the amount of thrust that the horse delivers against the ground. A western pleasure horse "steps" from one set of his diagonal pair of legs to the next diagonal pair, with little or no suspension between these steps. An English horse who thrusts against the ground with more energy lifts or suspends the legs momentarily between each diagonal pair of legs as he moves.

When a horse is loping, his legs move in three beats. If a horse is loping with four beats, he is said to be four beating. This is severely penalized because it means the horse is moving poorly and is not collected. A horse who is moving in the correct cadence receives credit for moving cleanly.

A western pleasure horse is penalized for excessive speed, wrong leads, break of gait, or overly high head carriage. Horses should be moving the body in a straight line. If a horse is canted at the lope with the

The trend of presenting the western pleasure horse with his head in an abnormally low position is being reversed by many breed organizations through rule changes that require judges to penalize this unnatural head and neck posture.

hip toward the center of the arena, out of line with his shoulders, the horse is penalized. Excessive opening of the mouth or nosing out are also undesirable traits.

Causes for disqualification are over flexing with the nose carried behind the vertical and the head held consistently too low. This makes the horse look intimidated and even if he is a good mover; this is a very undesirable trait.

In the past, western pleasure gained some bad notoriety due to horses looking thin, lethargic, too slow, and not moving at the prescribed beat for the gait desired.

Through the work of many horsemen and horsewomen who are involved in the major breed organizations, these traits have been recognized and dealt with. New rules were written into the rulebooks and the judges have been to seminars sponsored by the breed organizations. Education is the best way to make changes. Letting the public and the judges know what is to be expected has led to great strides in correcting what used to be wrong with western pleasure.

The popular event of western pleasure is an ever-changing class. As in any trendy sport, western pleasure is affected by new fads and fashions. Today, horses are bred specifically for the desired traits called for in the western pleasure classes, just as they are for reining and cutting. The horse who wins the western pleasure class should be the one who looks as the name implies—a pleasure to ride.

Chapter 7

Reining

with Linda Morse

Choreographed History

Reining is fast and fun, and it demands accuracy, emotional control, speed control, and riding skills. When you choose reining as a riding goal, you are also choosing many of the time-honored skills of western or cowboy traditions: honesty, personal fitness, balance, quiet confidence, compassion, understanding, and sportsmanship. The skills started as a necessity, used in the myriad jobs a horse and rider performed on a cattle ranch. Somewhere along the trail of history, one cowboy through his working horse was better than someone else's and what better way to spend a Sunday than to have a contest to see just who was right! Riders, proud of their horses' handle, met and rode off against one another, making the events into friendly contests between ranches. From that beginning the sport of reining has evolved into today's stylized display of training and skill, held in a *show pen.*

When it first became a horse show event, it was called a *stock horse* class. Now reining has moved from its ranch roots to the FEI level; the first western discipline to make it to the World Equestrian Games, it could easily become the first equestrian discipline under an Olympic flag with riders in western gear. It is considered by many to be the "classic" western discipline, and in the past century its popularity has spread throughout the

Reining is fast and fun.

world. The irony is that even in today's modern, mechanized climate, on ranches where quad runners cannot be used due to terrain or other issues, the horse still plays his traditional role of vital partner in the job of gathering and driving cattle, much the same way in which his ancestors did a hundred years ago and more.

To do the job, a horse must be athletic, maneuverable, quick, and responsive. Patterns or moves known as rollbacks, sliding stops, and spins must all be done with a great degree of control in order to keep cattle in a herd, catch a "stray," or move them across country without running the fat off them. This is a place where a hot shot rider, showing off by overriding his horse with rough aids, spurring and hauling on the bit, would be frowned upon and quickly ostracized by any true working cowboy.

Cutting, working cow horse, team penning, and team sorting are also contests that demonstrate the working or ranching skills of a horse and rider team. Ironically, the difference between these events and reining is that in reining you don't actually work with cattle. Originally the contest was designated as a dry stock horse class—*dry* meaning no cows. Today's show pen reiners perform an intricate dance with their horses, one that holds up a stylized mirror to the moves the ranch horse performs for a living. During the time the team is performing, they are being observed and scored by a panel of experienced judges. Today's top reining horses and young snaffle bit prospects can command prices in the six figures.

A Cautionary Tale

Reining requires dedication and athletic ability from both horse *and* rider, but it is one of the most fun things you can do on horseback. That being the case, it is hardly a surprise that many people new to horses and riding are attracted to the sport. A friend of mine got the reining bug and got into the discipline in just that way. She had gone to a show, seen some reining classes, and being a very athletic rider, assumed that if she bought a reiner, she would be one! So that is exactly what she did. I then watched as she got bucked off, run away with, and stomped on so many times I had the urge to call her Cat, but fortunately she ended up having more than nine lives. Unfortunately, she needed every one of them before her adventures in reining turned into an enjoyable experience. As one of her instructors, I cannot tell you how many times prayer was involved in her early lessons. What were the circumstances that led to such a life-threatening mistake? The answer is lack of awareness of what is required of the horse and rider as a team. She didn't understand how big a part she had to play in the partnership, so during her horse hunt, she concentrated her focus exclusively on looking for a horse who seemed to be able to do the work. She neglected to consider her responsibility for being able to ride that training. This is a common dilemma with the new, beginning, or novice rider: They don't know what they don't know!

Another missed fact that contributed to the less-than-desirable outcome to her purchase of this particular horse was that the horse was not a good match for her emotionally. While well trained, the horse was a worrier and became emotionally "volatile" when he couldn't understand his rider's cues. He was not the type of horse who accepted a rider's lack of position accuracy as simply human error and would carry on with the job he knew how to perform. Instead, the more confused he became, the hotter he got. Unfortunately for her, the trainer who sold her the horse did not take into account her lack of riding skills, or why those skills were needed with this particular gelding, who was "started" but not "made" (confirmed in his understanding and performance of his job to the point where he is confident in himself and relaxed, despite any inconsistencies in the rider). Moreover, when I assessed the gelding after she had purchased him, he appeared to have been rushed in his training. As a result, he had fear responses and lack-of-trust issues that made him unsuitable for a beginner and potentially dangerous in the wrong hands. He did not have a bad attitude; he was simply scared and did what any horse does by instinct: fight or try to flee. Since he was an athlete of reining caliber, he had the ability to do both; and did. Whether this was a case of unethical behavior (by a seller), a simple lack of attention to important details (on the part of the buyer), simple ignorance, or perhaps even wishful thinking by both buyer and seller, it should be remembered that this story exemplifies a situation that is not that uncommon in the horse world, no matter what the discipline.

To avoid this type of pitfall, which can be emotionally devastating if not outright physically dangerous, you (the buyer) need to understand your abilities and needs and that means doing your homework *before* you take the plunge. Even then the "buyer beware" statement holds true. But by getting an education and taking your time instead of rushing into a purchase, the chance of a bad outcome can be significantly reduced if not completely avoided. I am happy to report that with a lot of time, good coaching, and tenacity, the above horse and rider team actually worked out their problems. It took several years, and they were lucky, but they did indeed finally make it into the show pen.

The biggest problem I have witnessed over the years is that riders are in a hurry. Not big news (you hear it all the time), yet the difference between knowing something and doing something about it can a chasm as wide as the Grand Canyon, making self-control one of the most difficult skills to master in your journey toward excellence in any equestrian undertaking or discipline. The solution is very simple: if you want to rein, learn to ride first. But just because the concept is simple doesn't make it easy. Why? The ego is notoriously better than earplugs at making someone hard of hearing. I have seen far too many riders go into a specific discipline without first learning the basics of riding. By riding, I mean more than the ability to keep a leg on each side of the horse. You also have to learn to keep your mind in the middle, and that will take you more time than learning the basic skills of balance, feel, and timing.

Finding a Good Instructor

You want to start your exploration of the discipline of reining by finding a good riding instructor, one who understands biomechanics (how you and the horse work together), as well as the specifics of the discipline. Someone who can help you reach your goals in logical steps. For instance, riding a reiner is far more complex than one may realize because of the speed involved. You must first learn the skills of balance in order to be comfortable at speed. Then, once your body has adapted to that fear factor, you must train your mind to think at speed, learning to make the necessary observations and decisions about such things as how the horse is "shaped," or how well he is responding, or whether he is trying to get ahead of you. Before problems become major issues that mar your performance picture, you must correct them quickly as they arise, all by feel and technique. Find out more in the "Getting Help: Professional Training and Trainers" section later in this chapter.

Finding the Right Horse

Because the discipline of reining is definitely a partnership, finding just the right horse to join your team is as important as knowing how to ride well and memorizing the patterns of your class.

What Makes a Good Reiner?

Not every horse is suited to reining, but most horses can do at least part of what is required and can benefit from it. You may think that riding a circle is easy (dressage riders know better), until it is done as hard and as fast as your horse can go, and you have either a change of leads to execute or a stop with a set of spins in either direction, with style and timing integral to your score. You will also have to accept the fact that mistakes are made at every level, the pros included. You will forget a pattern here and there, and this is where the element of emotional control comes into play. As a rider, if you allow yourself to become distracted by your mistakes, or fall apart emotionally because of them during your ride, your timing and coordination will suffer, and thus the team's performance.

Thank goodness for technology and the information superhighway, as it converts the road of education from a cattle trail into a high-speed turnpike. I recommend that everyone take the trip on that road before buying a reiner. Videos, magazine articles, associations, and their Web sites are all available to help you familiarize yourself with the sport before you invest your money and time in a horse. Without this information, it is easy to set yourself up for very expensive and possibly life-threatening mistakes. The National Reining Horse Association (NRHA) Web site has all the patterns required for the sport, available for download at no charge. To this day I remember the response of one of the last students I started on the path of reining, when she went to the NRHA site for patterns. Just looking at the patterns sent her to the bathroom from nerves. Because she recognized her tendency to become overwhelmed mentally, she also trained herself to adopt a great philosophy about showing. Each time she entered the show pen she made it just her and her palomino horse against the pattern. Nothing else mattered but the two of them beating the pattern and besting their own last run. With this in mind, she learned to keep the pressure of competing at a level she could deal with, a very necessary thing if you want to succeed.

The National Reining Horse Association

Formed in 1966, the National Reining Horse Association (*www.nrha.com*) is the governing body for reining in America. This governing body is largely responsible for the sport of reining skyrocketing into current popularity. In 1994, Hollywood Jac 86 became the NRHA's first million-dollar sire. In 1995, Bill Horn was the first million-dollar (prize money) rider. In 1998, reining was accepted into USET, and 2005 saw Hollywood Dun It become the first $4 million sire. With million-dollar riders and horses to its credit, reining has come into its own as a serious sport, one that has Europeans coming to the United States to purchase competition prospects. Because Americans have been traveling abroad for more than a half century to purchase top-level dressage and jumping horses, it is great to have the trend reversed, and the economic impact for breeders and trainers of quarter horses could not be better.

Can My Horse Be a Reiner?

If you own a horse and want to get into reining, consider attending a clinic in order to expand your knowledge and test your horse's potential. There are general riding clinics, good for developing basic riding and performance skills, and there are reining clinics taught by discipline professionals. If the thought of putting yourself and your horse in the spotlight by riding in a clinic makes you nervous, take a wallflower approach by auditing, which is a great way to learn. It will also allow you to see how a particular trainer teaches, what his or her emphasis is, and whether it is geared to all riders or only to more experienced riders on show-ready horses. It can show you the "temperament" of the clinician. For every rider who learns well in a particular environment, there is a clinician who will suit your needs. In the past, I have ridden for hothead instructors; for passive, quiet types; and everything in between. Which one is best for you and or your horse may also vary with your experience in the game. In the beginning you will probably need an instructor who will give you confidence through a clinic structured in a way that ensures not only that you learn, but that you and your horse experience a reasonable amount of success. As you become more familiar with the discipline and get more competitive experience under your belt, you will probably want to work with a clinician who has a critical eye and can isolate and identify "holes" in you and/or your horse's performances, then tell you how to "fix" them. You'll have toughened up a bit through experience, so a clinician who is direct and blunt won't matter as long you get the important information that can improve your performance.

Before you start trying to turn your horse into a reiner, go to some shows sanctioned by the National Reining Horse Association. Watch not only the classes, but spend time watching what goes on at the warm-up pens. It is here you can often learn the most, as riders school their horses before going in to perform. You will have the opportunity to watch every level of rider, from the Green as Grass division riders to the Open Professionals.

Raising One of Your Own from Scratch

If you are thinking of breeding your own youngster to take up through the ranks, study pedigrees until you think you're going to go blind. People like Bob Loomis, Mike Boyle, and Shawn Flarida all have ideas about what lines are trainable, what lines produce the best open and amateur horses, and what lines improve with age and have a long career. Today's reiners are almost bionic. That is they are bred to stop, turn around, and have a good attitude in the process. Trainability is so critical to the pressure of reining in the show pen today it cannot be over-rated. Some of very recognizable sires—such as Top Sail Whiz, Hollywood Dun It, Smart Chic Olena, and foundation stallions like Joe Cody (sire of Topsail Cody)—should be in the pedigrees you look at. Look at the mare line as well. They can be up to 85 percent of what you end up with.

Buying a Reiner

If you are horseless or have a horse who is not suited to the show pen, but you have enough experience in the saddle to stay in the middle, execute simple tasks consistently (lead departs, simple stops, and so on), and have a rudimentary understanding of the terms used in the sport, then ask to take a lesson or two at a reining facility where you can ride an experienced horse. See if it is what you expected and how you get along with the instructor. See whether you're comfortable in the barn and see how you are treated by other students. If it is really intense the first time, go back a few times and make sure it wasn't just a bad day. Often the week before a show can be hectic, with riders going every which way in the arena, raised voices, everyone trying to get 'er done. If the program offered in that facility seems to suit you, and you need an entry-level horse, this is a good place to start. Ask the trainer/instructor to assist you in your search for a horse.

Soundness

Most good training barns will have horses for sale. Be sure you are looking at horses that are sound, good, and solid for entry-level reining. Experienced reiners who fill that bill may have miles on them, but if they are still serviceable, they are good teachers and can be good buys when fairly priced. These older, experienced, forgiving horses are the saints of the reining world. They carry you around while you learn and do not take the mistakes you are bound to make personally! They have the temperament to continue to do the job, even when you are still not able to be clear in what you ask. They may be somewhat arthritic due to the demands of the job, but with good shoeing and veterinary maintenance, they can have many good years left to teach you the ropes of the game. No matter what age horse you chose, do be prepared to spend the money on a thorough soundness exam. This should include radiographs, which can tell you what to expect from a particular animal. They can also tell you if there is anything major that may shorten your intended time on that first horse.

Expect to spend close to $500 or more for a complete exam. Consider the expense a form of insurance. When you are evaluating the findings on a older, experienced reiner, perhaps a bit past his prime, remember we are fortunate to live in an age where there is a great deal of technology available to help keep an old campaigner working and comfortable. Major advances in shoeing, pharmaceuticals, diagnostics, and alternative therapies have extended the lives of what I consider one of the greatest resources available to the novice: the seasoned horse. These can include daily feeding of chondroitin suflate and glucosamines, massage, BioScan, and chiropractic care, to name but a few. If you learn how to properly wrap legs, it can make a big difference to your old friend at the end of a hard show or even a hard work. Your vet can also use injectables of glucosamines and chondroitin sulfates on a regular basis to keep your horse's joints in a comfort zone.

Temperament

If your entry-level prospect is sound enough, then temperament is the next thing to consider. Even veterans can get a wild hair now and then. You'll want to be sure your riding skills are up to handling their occasional feel-good behavior. Remember even old campaigners were high-powered performers at some point. Most, however, are pretty kind, safe, and know their job (well enough to cheat on occasion). Have your instructor or trainer help you learn how to contain and correct such behavior, making you a better horseman in the process.

Conformation/Biomechanical Demands

There are some excellent videos out on good conformation (i.e., form to function). Study them and then go look at your horse(s) with an honest eye. Does a particular horse have low-set hocks or are they set high off the ground, and do you understand the biomechanical demands of your discipline enough to understand how this conformational aspect will affect your horse's performance and/or his long-term soundness? Is his natural neck set high, or is it low? How does it come out of the withers? Is his neck short and thick, or is it long and clean through the throat-latch, which would enable him to break easily at the poll? Does he have a strong hip and does it tie into his loin well? Is his back long or short? Can you divide him into equal thirds, using the triangle method? Is he heavier in his front end than his hindquarters? How big are his feet? Feet that are too small to offer good support for the muscular structure above can lead to early lameness issues, especially on horses who are subjected to the added training and performance "miles" necessary for showing. Is your horse reasonably straight in his front legs, not toeing out or in? When looking at him from the side, does he have an upright pastern or one that is too long? Does he bend at the knees well or is he tight? Too tight, and you could have tendon problems. When you watch your horse walk and trot away from you on a straight line, how do his feet land? Do they land heel first and straight? If not, you need to check if there is a shoeing problem and whether it can be fixed without compromising the future soundness of the horse. But if the good Lord made your horse to toe out, or in, thinking that you can change how his bones are put together could get you in trouble in the long haul. A horse who exhibits either of these traits to an extreme degree will be less likely to perform to a quality standard and also much more likely to break down prematurely. When looking at his hindquarters on a straight line, what do you see? Does he step under himself easily, not having too much rotation from the hip to the ground? Does he hit flat-footed here as well? Attending a conformation clinic or a course at your local college can help you to evaluate your present horse as well as educate you about what you want to be looking for in future purchases. All of these biomechanical factors can and do affect your horse's training, as well as his performance in the show ring and his longevity in the sport.

What to Pay

Deciding what a horse is worth depends on a number of factors. Knowing what his average score was when he was competing (for instance, it's good if he scored consistently in the low 70s), and knowing what division he competed in most often will give you an idea about the quality of competition he was matched against. Get ready to spend around $8,000 to $10,000 for a solid show horse for the Green as Grass level or for an older, semiretired campaigner. If that sounds like a lot of money, you may not be ready to play in this discipline.

Expand your knowledge of the degree of training (and its cost) that goes into producing a winner and the years it takes to produce that training, and you will begin to have a more realistic handle on what you can expect to pay for such a horse. That knowledge will also improve your chances of making your goal(s) attainable. As you consider what you want or can afford to invest in a reining horse, remind yourself that a good education is almost always more expensive than a poor one and what you are buying, at least in part, is an education (if you chose the right horse) because the horse will teach you over the next few years. If you think about it, it makes little sense to spend $40,000 on a truck to pull a $35,000 trailer with living quarters, but then to balk at paying for the years of education that a trainer has put in for a horse to become consistent in the show ring. Having said that, you can occasionally find a lesser-priced horse who will suit your needs, but if you do, my advice is to buy a lottery ticket the very same day—your luck is running hot!

Another option is to lease a horse. Certain circumstances may dictate that an owner has to take some time away from showing or riding. They may not want to part with "Ol' Slider" just yet, so they will allow someone else to use the horse in exchange for taking over expenses. A lease

A Reality Check

Being realistic in your evaluation of your own skills, your horse's skills, your goals, and your ability to follow through will go a long way toward ensuring your success over the years. Not expecting to purchase a Cadillac for the price of a skateboard is a good start.

If you find a good horse cheap, my advice is to buy a lottery ticket the same day—your luck is running hot!

agreement can be a win-win situation for both you and the horse owner because it gives you, the rider, a chance to ride a seasoned horse until you can find or afford your own. Almost always there will be a clause about insurance and staying with a particular trainer. This guarantees to the horse owner that continuity and a certain level of care will be maintained for Ol' Slider. The beauty of leases is that they can be tailored to each party involved. Normally you, the person leasing, can expect the following expenses to be included: boarding, shoeing, vet bills, insurance, showing fees, and training and/or lesson fees. In exchange you get to ride a super athlete without spending huge amounts of money up front. Some leases can be as short as ninety days; some can be open-ended depending on everyone's circumstances. You are most likely to find a horse to lease through a trainer, or in a discipline-specific training barn.

When you do find yourself the owner of a great horse, insure him if you could not go out and replace him. In the event he becomes ill or injured to the point of needing surgery, you don't want to have to be in the position of asking the vet to euthanize your buddy because the cost of surgery is more than you can afford. Nor do you want to have to start saving for another four or five years before you can afford to buy another horse of the same caliber.

Getting Help: Professional Training and Trainers

Reining is like art—as with dressage, it takes time, perfect practice, and a good support network of trainer, vet, farrier, instructor, horse, family, and friends if you and your horse are to rise to the top. When you see the professionals, know that their start in the sport was probably a lot like yours. A good professional can be a great asset, playing the role of your advisor, your cheerleader, your confessor, and your disciplinarian. If you want to show beyond schooling shows, you will definitely need to consider working with a good trainer. Good riders are usually made, not born, and while every professional has something to offer, realize that not every trainer may be the right one for you and your horse. In order to find the best for your particular combination, you will need to be an informed consumer during your hunt. You may also have to travel, and you will certainly have to invest some money when you find the right trainer or the right training barn.

There are as many theories on how to train a reining horse as there are in any other show ring discipline. All good horses are *in balance:* straight, able to bend any part of their body with a light touch of rein or leg. Well-trained horses will let you direct the placement of their head, neck, shoulders, ribs, hips, and feet willingly, with light aids. Many of today's horses exhibit a naturally low head carriage, which makes *framing* (getting the horse to carry itself in an efficient and therefore maximized athletic posture when he is being ridden) so much easier. These want to carry themselves round with their hind ends set up under themselves. Yes, you have to train them to stay there at all gaits, and to carry their weight evenly between their front end and their back end when in motion, but as a group this type of a horse is much easier to train. Fighting conformation is a losing battle.

Look at the industry's top trainers' horses. True, styles in the show pen come and go with the years, but the stayers know you can't force a horse into a style very long before the horse shuts down and simply won't perform. Good trainers will look for feedback from their horses, allowing a horse to have some say in the physical frame they are the most comfortable with during their work. Some horses will prefer to travel with their nose slightly in front of vertical; some will want to elevate their necks a bit for better balance during a stop. Some horses will want to stick their nose out during a spin and can still take the small steps during a spin that will garner them a plus for the maneuver. As a trainer once told me, all it takes is 217 years to learn all that. So as you assess and evaluate the trainers and the horses they are riding, considering not only their recent show results but also the longevity of their show records will be of benefit in your self-education and fact-finding mission. Sound like a lot of homework? It is, but winning requires work, not just skill and/or good luck.

If you have a horse who hasn't been started, you will most likely need to invest in the services of a trainer. Unless you are very experienced at starting babies, it is a job best left to the professionals. Nothing is harder than to undo a bad start, especially if you have a specific discipline in mind. Your pocketbook and peace of mind are at stake when purchasing a horse for a specialized discipline such as reining. You'll want to be able to expect a successful career with this horse, so taking the necessary steps to insure both you and your horse get the best start possible only makes good sense. Be prepared to hear some occasional bad news; for any number of reasons, the baby you picked may not be the right one for you at this point in your riding career or be the best one to take you to your intended competition goals. If you tend to kill the messenger of this type of news, don't be surprised when people are not willing to tell you the truth, the whole truth, and nothing but the truth. But the truth can save you time, a ton of money, and the less than joyful experience of moving from one frustrating roadblock to another. Instead, learn to thank the professional who may be trying to save you money and grief, and if you do not feel confident of the accuracy of that particular person's opinion or evaluation, spend some time talking to a few other trainers, and evaluate carefully what you hear before you make any decisions. Not every trainer is right for every horse, and conversely, not every owner is right for every trainer. Most riders end up using a trainer within an hour or two of where they live. Although the convenience of proximity is important to anyone who works, has a family, and wants to ride and compete, you should not select a trainer based solely on the fact that his or her barn is located right down the road from where you live. Instead, spend time watching those trainers at their home barn and at shows within a reasonable distance. Watch to see how they work, not only with horses but with their students as well.

At a show, everything changes. The pressure is on everyone there to have a good run. Often I have seen the amateurs stress more than the pros. Remember that the pros are paid to produce so they have pressure on them that you, the amateur rider, never will have to cope with. The warm-up arenas are unlike anything you have experienced at home. There is a different set of etiquette, rules, and courtesy at either its finest or its worst. You need to see and learn what that is and how to cope with the extra stress put on you and your horse. Most riders find it very intimidating at the beginning of their show career. A good trainer will help you learn the behavior protocols appropriate in this type of situation. A good trainer and his or her clients should also put at least some emphasis on having fun while you are there—a fact that is easily lost during the pressure of showing.

If you have to work forty hours a week and have family obligations, you may want leave your horses in training or partial training year round. However, if you prefer to have your horse return home with you after his initial time with your trainer, you can haul in for lessons with your trainer each week and periodically put your horse back with your trainer for a "tune-up." A good time for a tune-up is before show season, or in the middle of the show season. By allowing your trainer exclusive time in the saddle, he or she can evaluate the subtle things in a horse's work that can get you into trouble in the very near future, or may tell him you are doing a fine job maintaining your horse's performance on your own. Unless you are very experienced, most horses will benefit from a pro sitting on them now and then. Another way for you and your horse to benefit from the services of your trainer is to have your trainer occasionally show your horse in a class. This can produce a mountain of information about the horse, for both you and your trainer. A good trainer might deliberately chose to throw away a chance to ribbon your horse in a particular class in order to do what they feel might be necessary corrective schooling to keep your horse honest in the show pen. This practice is sometimes necessary because really smart horses may figure out a way to cheat in the show pen because they learn the rider can't respond to the horse's behavior (or lack of it) in the same firm, corrective way they would were they schooled at home. A horse can quickly learn he can drop a shoulder during a spin, lean into a change of leads, shorten a stop, rush a rollback, and so on. A good trainer must take the opportunity to correct such behaviors at that moment in order to impress upon the horse that he must adhere to a specific standard of performance *at all times*. Failure to do that opens the door for the issue, whatever it is, to become a much bigger problem when the money is down. A good trainer or instructor will also teach you how to do the same thing both at home and at a show. If your goal is to move from the entry level of Green as Grass to Rookie and on up the ladder, you are working for longevity in your horse's performance, not just the immediate gain of a placing in a class.

No horse will stay trained if you are riding the training out of your horse every time you mount up. That is why the process of finding and selecting a professional you respect and one who works well with you and your horse is an important ingredient in the sport of reining, especially if you and your horse want to succeed in the show pen.

At training barns with quality programs, I see plenty of support for students both in the warm-up arenas and ringside during a class. And at the end of the day, no matter who won or who lost, it seemed the barn as a whole had fun in the process. I've seen riders and coaches from a particular barn who are still at ringside at nearly midnight, just to lend the support of their presence to the last rider of the day from their barn, riding in her first class. That kind of dedication shows me that the student matters, no matter their level of experience or performance ability. Whether it is your first show or you have been doing it for years, that type of support is often the ingredient that makes showing a richly rewarding experience for the amateur owner.

Some trainers may not want to work with you and your particular horse if they do not feel they can be of value to you. Those circumstances might include a horse who does not have the mental ability to handle the training pressure, one who physically cannot do the job (and therefore shuts down), or one who does not work well with beginning reiners. Trainers must first be honest with themselves before they can be honest with you, the customer. So find one who seems to suit you and your horse, then talk to current and past customers. Watch for show results in the many magazines that feature the discipline and explore Web sites geared to reining.

Although trainers are paid to produce results for their clients, either with the client's horses or for you as a rider on your own horse, they should keep a good perspective on why you, the student, are there in the first place. And the good ones do. Having watched the Boyle Ranch in the recent past, I saw plenty of great support for their students in both the warm-up arenas and ringside during a class. And it seemed that the whole barn had fun. Everyone not showing or warming up is at ringside to cheer on the barn buddies in a class.

Basic Reining Work for Your Horse

The trick to learning basic reining is to take everything slowly in the beginning. If you are working with a professional, be sure they know that your goal for the particular horse you are on currently might not be the show pen, but rather his use as a practice horse to let you get a sense of what all of the fuss is about. Introducing and practicing the reining moves hopefully will engage and lighten your partner. While some horses may have physical limitations, either from conformation or work-related issues, you can start out learning to "feel" a good circle, an entry-level rollback, a simple change of leads, a balanced stop on any horse you have at present. While you may not get big dramatic sliding stops, or super-fast turnarounds, you can gain an incredible amount of feel and under-standing on your average horse, so that when you make your next step up, you are ready to refine what they have taught you. In fact, if we accept their limitations as well as our own, the horses that usually teach us the most are first horses and those who aren't perfect or easy. If you have practiced, taken lessons, and learned your patterns, you can progress to a local schooling show. Not all will have reining classes, but some do, and this is a good environment in which to get your feet wet for the first time. If you are not yet ready to compete in recognized reining shows, you will not need to worry about points. But make sure that you are not jeopard-izing a future show status (i.e., Amateur, Green as Grass, and so on) by showing at a local show. A trainer or a coach should be able to advise you here, but it is also your responsibility to become familiar with the rules that apply to your discipline set down by its governing body. If you are currently trying to "go it alone," this tip by itself could easily be worth the price of this book in helping you avoid becoming accidentally dis-qualified from a division at some time in the future.

The Show Pen Experience

According to the NRHA handbook, "To rein a horse is not only to ride him, but control his every movement." In scoring, "smoothness, finesse, attitude, quickness and authority" are the qualities a judge looks for.

Looking at Reining Patterns

All reining patterns require the following maneuvers. How they are per-formed dictates your score. You can plus or minus a maneuver either by doing it in a spectacular manor (plus) or in a manner that the judges feel could have been better (minus). All riders start with a score of 70 but can score from 0 to "infinity" depending on the quality of the work presented. Judges can add or deduct up to 10 points in increments of a half point, with major deviations resulting in a 0 or no score.

- **Circles** are to be round, not oval or egg-shaped, and should start and end at the same point. They are to be exactly as called for. Small circles are usually executed in a slow or collected lope; large are usually executed at a fast yet controlled gallop. Variations of speed as called for in a pattern can be a way to plus your work *if* you can get true speed control and a definite change from fast to slow.

- **Flying changes** (of the leading leg) in reining have progressed to the point where they are often a hind foot first change. That, as in dressage, is the prettiest, but a front foot first change is acceptable in reining (unlike in dressage). The difference can be best seen and studied on video in slow motion. The changes have to be on the mark, at the center of the circle(s), and should be done in a smooth manner, without the horse "leaning" into the new lead, or increasing his speed, and with subtle body cues from the rider.

- **Spins, or turnarounds,** should be done as smoothly as possible, with the horse's inside hind foot staying in place. Generally, a judge would want to see the spin "flat" and done through the trot, with small steps. Depending on the horse's particular style, one would like to see the outside front foot either cross over or step to the inside front foot. If you see a horse stepping his outside front foot behind the inside front foot, beware because the horse could be considered "backing" through his spin, and will loose points in a competition. In the early days of reining, spins were most often done at the canter and resulted in more of a hopping motion than the spins we see today. The speed you see on the great ones comes only after the footwork is confirmed. If you are trying spins with your horse at home, do not worry about speed. Videotaping your work will be invaluable to you when you are learning.

- **Rollbacks** are just that, rolling back away from the direction of travel. It is done toward the fence, back to the new direction. To be done well, it incorporates a stop with a very small amount of hesitation to prepare the horse for the turn. You are allowed to come out on the incorrect lead, but you must change to the correct lead before you reach the new corner. I see this happen a lot and while you cannot be penalized if you change the lead as described above, it does present a much cleaner look if the correct lead is taken at the completion of the turn. The better rollbacks are accomplished as described with "a touch of the rein on the neck." The stop cannot be a complete stop since the horse would lose momentum, and the maneuver is to be done as one single move, not two.

- **Sliding stops** are the crowd pleasers. They are dramatic and heart-stopping to see as well as to do, and are usually the last part of the pattern. To be done well, the horse has to gradually accelerate its speed, the rider maintaining complete control, and then when the team is near or at the "marker" (orange cones placed along the side wall at the middle and both ends of the arena), the rider asks the horse to stop. What we all want to see and feel is the hind end well up under the horse, the front end still moving, still running, the head and neck soft and in balance. What we don't want to see or feel is the front end *locking up;* in other words, stiff legged stops with the horse throwing his head up in the air and his mouth pulled open. Good balanced stops are a joy to behold and an even bigger thrill to ride. Most of today's well-bred reiners are bred to stop and have the confirmation to do it easily. But the maneuver still requires proper training and correct riding, or your horse will pay the price in soundness.

Running over the judge will cost you minus points on your reining score.

There are literally hundreds of questions that you will learn to ask yourself over time. Here are a few really important ones:

- Did I complete the pattern?

- Did I really show a change of speed?

- Did I make each and every move at the required spot?

- Did I rush my horse on a rollback?

- Did I rush my horse on a stop?

- Did I make really round circles?

- Were my large and fast circles large and fast?

- Were my small and slow circles really just that?

- How did my horse feel during warm-up?

- Did I leave my best moves in the warm-up pen?

- Did I watch my competitors and then suddenly try to change my way of working my horse because they were doing something I thought might be better?

While we would all like to plus every maneuver, understand that every horse has its strong and weak points. So if you have a horse who is a great stopper but has some limitations on spins, your training program should be designed to improve your horse's weak areas, but also capitalize on his best points. A trainer would be a good resource for help with such evaluation and work. The beauty of reining scoring is that, like dressage, each movement is assigned its own score, and if you or your horse blow it on one maneuver, you still have the rest of the pattern to try and plus. The hardest thing for the entry-level reiner is to not panic if one part of the pattern turns out badly. When that happens, you can often forget where you are in the pattern, quit riding your horse well at the point of the mistake, and think that the whole class is blown and make a big mistake.

You will learn quite a bit about yourself during your first trip in a reining pattern. Most of you will not be able to come out of the arena and describe in detail how each of your required moves was executed, what you could have done to make them better, where you went off course (if you did), whether you hit your "markers," and what you think you may have scored. And these are things you really need to know as you increase your abilities and improve your performance and scores. All I ever hoped for when I had a first timer was that nobody came out scared, hurt, or feeling like a failure. If you survived, you were a winner, because you tried.

NRHA Reining Pattern 2

Horses may walk or trot to the center of arena. Horses must walk or stop prior to starting pattern. Begin at the center of the arena facing the left wall or fence.

1. Beginning on the right lead, complete three circles to the right: the first circle small and slow, the next two circles large and fast. Change leads at the center of the arena.

2. Complete three circles to the left: the first circle small and slow, the next two circles large and fast. Change leads at the center of the arena.

3. Continue around previous circle to the right. At the top of the circle, run down the middle to the far end of the arena past the end marker and do a right rollback—no hesitation.

4. Run up the middle to the opposite end of the arena, past the end marker, and do a left rollback—no hesitation.

5. Run past the center marker and do a sliding stop. Back up to the center of the arena or at least ten feet. Hesitate.

6. Complete four spins to the right. Hesitate.

7. Complete four spins to the left. Hesitate to demonstrate the completion of the pattern.

Rider must dismount and drop the bridle to the designated judge.

Pattern 2

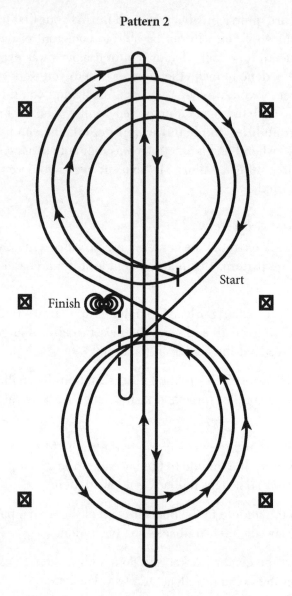

NRHA Reining Pattern 6

Horses may walk or trot to the center of arena. Horses must walk or stop prior to starting pattern. Begin at the center of the arena facing the left wall or fence.

1. Complete four spins to the right. Hesitate.

2. Complete four spins to the left. Hesitate.

Pattern 6

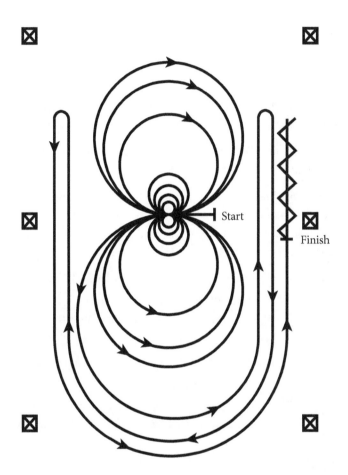

3. Beginning on the left lead, complete three circles to the left: the first two circles large and fast, the third circle small and slow. Change leads at the center of the arena.

4. Complete three circles to the right: the first two circles large and fast, the third circle small and slow. Change leads at the center of the arena.

5. Begin a large fast circle to the left but do not close this circle. Run up the right side of the arena past the center marker and do a right rollback at least 20 feet from the wall or fence—no hesitation.

Riding Tips to "Plus" Pattern 6

Maneuver 1: To plus this requirement, make your spins start and end *exactly* at the same point. Accuracy is more important than sloppy speed.

Maneuver 2: Same as above.

Maneuver 3: *Perfect* circles, marked change in speed, and a smooth lead change give you several chances to plus this portion.

Maneuver 4: The beginning and end of *each* circle should be at the same exact spot to plus this set of maneuvers.

Maneuver 5: Make sure to go past the marker, then make the rollback *one* smooth move. Getting your horse's hind end well up him will help give you a dramatic slide *into* the rollback, which can help impress a judge.

Maneuver 6: Coming out of your first rollback in the correct lead, consistent speed, and making sure to stay the required 20 feet away from the fence can be worth plus points here.

Maneuver 7: This is your last chance to impress the judge, so making sure of where your marker is, get a straight, long slide, then flow into the backup with minimal rein pressure to garner your plus points.

6. Continue back around previous circle but do not close this circle. Run up the left side of the arena past the center marker and do a left rollback at least 20 feet from the wall or fence—no hesitation.

7. Continue back around previous circle but do not close this circle. Run up the right side of the arena past the center marker and do a sliding stop at least 20 feet from the wall or fence. Back up at least 10 feet. Hesitate in order to demonstrate the completion of the pattern.

Rider must dismount and drop the bridle to the designated judge.

NRHA Reining Pattern 9

In the following section you find an explanations of the maneuvers of reining pattern 9, movement by movement.

1. Run past the center marker and do a sliding stop. Back up to the center of the arena or at least ten feet. Hesitate.

2. Complete four spins to the right. Hesitate.

3. Complete four and one-quarter spins to the left so that horse is facing the left wall or fence. Hesitate.

Pattern 9

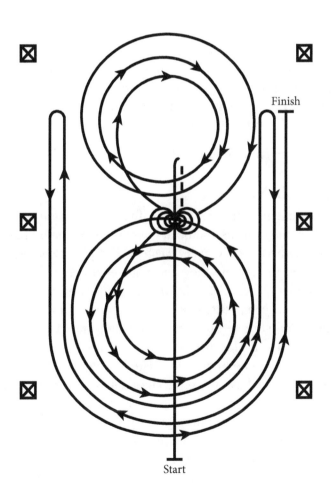

4. Beginning on the left lead, complete three circles to the left: the first circle small and slow, the next two circles large and fast. Change leads at the center of the arena.

5. Complete three circles to the right: the first circle small and slow, the next two circles large and fast. Change leads at the center of the arena.

6. Begin a large fast circle to the left but do not close this circle. Run up the right side of the arena past the center marker and do a right rollback at least 20 feet from the wall or fence—no hesitation.

7. Continue back around the previous circle but do not close this circle. Run up the left side of the arena past the center marker and do a left rollback at least 20 feet from the wall or fence—no hesitation.

8. Continue back around the previous circle but do not close this circle. Run up the right side of the arena past the center marker and do a sliding stop at least 20 feet from the wall or fence. Hesitate to demonstrate completion of the pattern.

Rider must dismount and drop the bridle to the designated judge.

Dealing with Nerves

Show nerves are a huge thing to tackle. To be able to ride your warm-up in the show pen the same as you do at home is a monumental task. I have seen riders lose their cool in every western discipline, change their program at the last minute, and blow their horses up. Your horse has been used to you doing things a certain way for six months to a year. You go to a show, see your competitors, see trainers, and your emotions get you by the throat. You start trying to ride like someone else and your poor horse does not have a clue who you are and what is going on! Where did the rider go whom he knew and trusted? Then all of a sudden, your program—the one you have worked so hard on—is gone and you couldn't find it with a search warrant, so you get even more worried, and then Ol' Slider gets more worried, and the war is on. The emotional control issue has reared its ugly head! What do you do now? Ride off into a corner, *breathe*, smile, and know that this is just *one* day, *one* ride, *one* class in your life, and win, lose, or draw, you can spin another day, no matter what. Judges are there to give you an opinion for that one ride; they are not there to evaluate your whole life. Keep it in perspective. You started this journey because it looked like fun, remember? Keep that in mind now. Early in my career, I asked a trainer how long it would take me to learn whatever it was I was trying to learn at that point in my riding. He answered, "Two hundred and seventeen years and you will never be perfect, so now that you know that, quit worrying and have fun." It was one of the best pieces of advice I've ever received.

Getting the Right Equipment

When you go to a show, your equipment list will include some of the following items, indigenous to reiners and reining:

- **Front boots or bandages:** The boots come in an array of styles, but the priority here is protection of the ligaments and tendons.

- **Skid boots:** These protect your horse's hind ankles during his rundowns. If you "burn" your horse's ankles, he may start to refuse to stop or may shorten his stop.

- **Bell boots:** These are put on your horse's front feet to protect him from grabbing himself on his spins.

- **Western saddle:** This type of saddle is usually plain, especially when compared to the ones used by the western pleasure and equitation crowd. It must be clean, and in absolutely good repair. Most riders have one saddle for work and one for show.

- **Bridles:** Single ear, split ear, or full brow bands are a matter of style preference. You can get away with more "dress up" here for your horse and can enhance a pretty head or make a plain one prettier. The more silver the more dollars, so let your pocketbook be your guide, but know that no amount of silver will plus your stop or spin!

Ladies' dress is neat and tidy, but sequins and flash aren't usually a part of the well-dressed reiners wardrobe. The gents' dress is simple and conservative.

Make sure your equipment is clean, not dusty or caked with dried sweat. It is a sign of respect for your horse, the judge, and the sport. That first impression you make as you enter the gate and ride to the judge is the only first impression you get that day. Make it count!

Caring for Your Horse at the Show

When it comes to the hands-on care for your horse during your time at a show, I am a bit old-fashioned in my feelings about doing everything you can for the horse to keep him comfortable and sound and happy so that he will not hate his job.

At the end of a day, no matter whether it was a one-day or a multi-day event, I always rub down the horse's legs with either alcohol or some sort of brace made for the purpose. That little extra time can give you the opportunity to notice if your horse has a sore tendon, heat in a leg, or any cuts. We are asking the horse to be a professional athlete. Think about what goes on in a ballplayers' locker room after a game: massages, hot tubs, showers, liniment, and so on. A myriad of topical ointments, gels, and rubs are available, but the day of a show is not the time to use a product for the first time. If your horse has a bad reaction to a substance, you don't want to find out at a show, so use only what you have first used at home. Some products on the market may contain ingredients that have been banned as performance enhancing. It is your duty to know this information before you go to a show. A list of those substances can be obtained from USEF, the governing body for all horse sports in America. It is then your responsibility to read the labels of the products you use and to know the ingredients.

If you are in a show barn, do not expect the trainer or the hired help to take care of these matters. It is your horse, your investment, and your responsibility to do the "extras" for your equine athlete. Get educated! Have someone teach you how to wrap legs. Done incorrectly, wrapping can cripple a horse. You'll want to introduce bandages to your horse at home so he has time to learn to tolerate them being left on. Some horses may try to chew them off. You also need to know that your horse will not kick the wall of his stall all night long in an attempt to get the unfamiliar things off his legs.

You can simply hose down your horse and put him away for the day, but a little preventative maintenance can be a valuable thing in the long run. A warm bath with a follow-up of some warm alcohol or a body brace can make your horse a happy one. Icing legs with some of the great ice boots available to us now can cool hot legs and keep minor soreness from becoming a major problem. Even hosing the horse's legs down for fifteen to twenty minutes will help hot tissues cool out more quickly. Of course, you need the normal brushes, hoof picks, mane and tail combs, conditioner, and other things that go with any "show" scene, but my arsenal is a lot bigger. Taking care of your partner in this way, you get to spend some quiet time reflecting on the day's events, how your run went, and what you need to do for the next day. I've noticed that during this quiet care time, I can really get to know where my horse is mentally at the end of a hard day. It's a great way of saying thank you for his efforts, made at my request.

The Stop Sign Drill

One of the simplest, yet most effective reining drills I've ever encountered was introduced to me by reining trainer Pat Wyse, who used the drill during a clinic at my facility. As I watched the various riders work the following pattern, its versatility and effectiveness were quickly evidenced by the improvement in each horse and rider.

- *Exercise focus:* to make short, straight lines from one point in your arena to the next. Use cones or buckets to mark the "corners" of your octagon pattern (think "stop sign"). Eventually all the lines you ride should become the same length, creating the "stop sign" pattern.

- *Exercise effects:* your horse's ability to "stand up," follow his nose with his whole body, and move his shoulders *only* when and as much as his rider is requesting him to.

- *Exercise benefits:* precise control over the diameter of a circle, no matter what its size, while maintaining a consistent rate of speed is essential in order to perform a winning reining pattern.

Start by visualizing the octagon—short, straight lines, eight sides. Pick a starting point and ask your horse to get straight between the reins as you proceed at walk toward your chosen point. Do not help the horse by using any leg aids. Rather, just set your hands evenly on the reins, which you will hold slightly away from his neck to either side. The reins will form a shallow "V" with the horse's mouth at the point of the V. As you allow the horse to walk toward the spot you have chosen, he may "ping pong" between the reins, until he finds where "straight" is. When he is straight, what you will feel in your hands is "lightness." When your horse is leaning or not straight, you will feel a heaviness on one rein or the other, or he will seem to be "pulling" on you. When the horse straightens himself and becomes balanced between your reins, release the pressure by sliding your hands slightly forward toward the bit. Allow the horse to walk a distance before you change the line, or change direction.

To change the line of the octagon, tip the horse's nose toward the new line and again wait until the horse finds his new straight line. At the beginning of your exercise, your lines will most likely be uneven. That's okay. The point of this is to let the horse find that new line; let him find that when he is straight, all the pressure is released. If you help him in the initial stages by adding too much leg or spur, you will complicate his learning curve. You may actually slow his learning and cause the horse distress by giving him too much data to process. Repeat this drill three to four times a week until your horse understands what is asked of him and is consistent in his response to you. It is not uncommon to have five or fewer "lines" in the beginning, some longer than others depending on how well your horse "gets it," so don't fret. Don't forget you will want to train your horse through the exercise both clockwise and counterclockwise.

When your horse has accomplished this stage of the exercise, you will move him up to the next gait and repeat the learning process. If you've built a solid foundation at the walk, your horse will respond much more quickly to the demands of the exercise at the jog or trot. After you're schooled at all three gaits in both directions, the next step in the training exercise will be to make the octagon smaller. Don't be discouraged if you find that you have to start from the beginning because of the smaller diameter. Remember, while your horse may now understand what you are asking of him, by making the training pattern tighter (smaller), you are also challenging his strength and balance to a great degree and it will take time for him to adapt to these greater demands on his systems. It is always a good training practice to go back to a slower gait if you find your horse struggling with any drill. Faster will not make it better; it will tend to make it worse. Your horse's success at understanding what is asked of him—the basics—must always be refined in order to have your "finish" be what you need in the show pen.

All contest patterns consist of basic moves (basic training), put together in a finished, prescribed pattern. The drill can also become part of your daily checklist. By doing it for a short time during each ride as you warm up your horse, you will learn if your horse is working evenly on both sides, or if he is hanging on the bit more on one side than on the other. It will tell you if he is keeping his shoulders straight (rather than leaning) and if he is tracking up with the inside hind leg through the change of line. This is a great drill for any discipline, creating a well-balanced horse.

Winning Is All About Attitude

Getting someone to videotape you while you are riding is one of the absolutely best ways to get in touch with reality. There is no more valuable tool to see what you are doing at any given point in your routine. Learn to evaluate yourself honestly—critically, yes, but also fairly—and you will quickly find yourself moving way ahead of the competition. The most profound moment I ever had was during a taped working session at a clinic with Monte Foreman. Monte was getting on in years at the time, and his vision had become a bit compromised, or so I thought. In my job as trainer that year, I was riding a number of my clients' hunt seat horses, so I had apparently gotten into the habit of carrying my upper body in a forward position. For the work Monte wanted from me, I needed to be sitting up, carrying my shoulders directly above my hips. During the clinic I kept hearing him say over and over, "Get your shoulders back!" I just knew that the old man couldn't possibly see, since I felt as though I had moved my upper body so far back I was lying on my mare's tail! About that time, thoughts of my having a not-so-good clinic began running through my head. Then, during lunch break, we watched the video of my ride. Well, that video kicked my attitude hard! There I was, big as brass, and *every* time Monte said, "Get your shoulders back over your butt," my response was to lift my chin. It felt to me like I had done what he was asking, but I hadn't.

Years later, I would hear a clinician talk about how a rider's kinesthetic sense could become distorted, preventing the rider from being truly aware of what they were doing on a horse. I remembered my clinic experience with Monte. I would have bet everything I owned on Monte's vision being at fault, and it was a revelation to me to learn that my brain could *lie* to me about where my body was located in physical space. The death of my ego on that day opened the door fully to my desire to improve and also to be open to learning. I didn't fail to notice that in order to gain that next step up the ladder of knowledge, I had to first learn how to become humble.

Monte Foreman: A Man Ahead of His Time

Monte Foreman was a pioneer whom I was most fortunate and most grateful to meet when I was a kid with a burning desire—but no experience—to go fast and do the "tricks" I had seen at my first big show, the Grand National Livestock and Horseshow in San Francisco, California.

He was one of the first, if not the very first, to use film in order to study the biomechanics of his sport and its riders and horses. As he studied the performance of horses in the stock classes in the early 1940s, he realized that the way in which riders rode and trained their horses was actually preventing the horse from attaining his athletic potential in this particular field. What a concept! Today you will hear this common theme all the time from well-known clinicians at the large equine expos such as the Western States Horse Expo on the West Coast and the Equine Affair expos in the Midwest and on the East Coast. But Monte was the first one to make the statement, and to break down movement and the analysis of horse and rider and the equipment used in the sport of reining.

Through trial and error, massive amounts of research, and working with professionals such as the great Jimmy Williams, he discovered that if we wanted the harmony seen in today's reiners, the rider had to learn to work *with* the horse, not against him. This led to the design and development of equipment such as the "balanced ride" saddle, which made it easier for the horse and rider to move as one balanced unit while executing a series of training exercises; he later called this "The Basic Handle." In his attempt to educate the general riding public, he made films, wrote magazine articles and books, and spent most of his entire life on the road giving clinics in which he taught others what he himself had learned through years of intensive study.

I started riding with Monte in 1965 and rode with him until he passed away. The last time I had the privilege of watching him ride was in 1981, at his ranch in Colorado. My best reining buddy and I were moved to tears as we watched this great horseman and teacher put his foot in the stirrup, pull his old body up onto his thoroughbred, Sir Patrick, and execute the prettiest hind foot first changes of lead that anyone has ever produced. The lightness and harmony we witnessed that day, which were espoused by Monte throughout his career, paved the way for the "natural horsemanship" we see so much of today. His system of training is carried on by his students, trainers such as Pat Wyse, who co-authored Monte's last book. He was far ahead of his time, and his approach to the issues of his craft were often considered radical. His patience with riders was huge. He gave me a foundation for my entire career, one that utilized reining concepts to make any horse a better athlete—from rail horses to sour dressage horses to starting colts. In turn, I have spent my lifetime passing this on to my own clients for the benefit of their horses.

Chapter 8

Western Speed and Skill Contests

with Linda Huck

The History of Gymkhana

Games on horseback have been a part of history since mankind first trained and rode the horse. The ancient Greeks practiced drills where men rode in columns and then dispersed into circles. The Romans had chariot races, and their cavalry practiced their sword thrusts on the palus (a wooden post set up in the training area). The knights in King Arthur's court jousted to win the court's favor. The Austrian Hussars rode at a gallop as they attempted to spear artificial turban-wrapped heads with their lances, and the Native Americans played games on horseback to prove their strength and worth.

The term *gymkhana* (jim-KAH-nah) first appeared in East India during the British Colonial period, when the Indian soldiers rode in athletic contests or games. They called their riding exercises gymkhanas, meaning a place where contests of skill are held. The soldiers realized that by performing these "games," their horses became more agile, their reactions were sharpened, and both horse and rider became more physically fit. The horse and rider also developed a feeling of mutual trust. The Indian Soldiers had an exceptionally good sense of balance and quickly became at ease on their mounts. In turn, their horses became responsive to the lightest of touches and were quite able to tackle whatever was required of them. The British, realizing how valuable these exercises were, soon started incorporating gymkhana exercises into their own training and sporting activities.

Today gymkhana is a worldwide discipline that has taken on many different forms. Timed events such as barrels, poles, keyhole, and various other patterns test the strength, speed, and balance of horse and rider. Some require the horse to gallop for short distances, or jump small obstacles, but all of these games evolved for the purpose of improving horsemanship and encouraging trust between horse and rider.

Although there are numerous gymkhana events, barrel racing is probably the most popular and well-known event in the United States today. Not only is barrel racing included in gymkhana events, but it is an exciting rodeo event as well. Some of the top contenders in barrel racing are now winning as much prize money as the rough stock (bull and bronc) riders. Junior rodeos have barrel racing and pole bending also.

Numerous organizations, such as the California Gymkhana Association, promote these activities throughout the United States and around the world. Gymkhanas are fun for any age group, and the competitive classes at some events are divided by age and experience, where you won't have to go supersonic to win. This is where novice horse and rider teams can start.

What to Look for in Speed Games' Horses

One of the most important elements I look for in a prospect is natural athleticism. While any horse can be trained to perform gymkhana patterns, I prefer to start with one who has a natural ability to move gracefully, over one who is clumsy or tends to trip over his own feet. When looking at a prospective horse, I want to watch him moving free before a saddle is placed on his back and a rider climbs aboard, since an unbalanced rider or a poorly fitting saddle can alter a horse's movement quite a bit.

In the roping events, I notice whether the horse seems interested in the cattle or whether they're fearful or resistant to working with them. When Bombay, my awesome Arabian, first saw cattle, he really wasn't too thrilled about the notion of getting in there and moving around among them. But with time and patience he came to love chasing cattle.

During a practice roping session, a friend, who is an older rancher and diehard quarter horse person, rode up to me and said, "Don't tell anyone I said this, but that little horse of yours is going great and working cattle nicely." Knowing his preference in breeds, I was pleased when he complimented my little horse and knew my horse was "doing well" to earn such praise from a "critic."

On the other hand, I had a dapple-gray Arabian, Kouros, who would work cattle but didn't really enjoy it. His favorite thing to do was wait until my attention was totally focused on the steer we were chasing and then start bucking. When this happened at a team penning, he went to bucking for almost the whole length of the arena before he gave it up. I decided it was his way of telling me that he wasn't enjoying his work. He excelled in English disciplines and was a good trail horse; he just wouldn't tolerate working around cattle.

Correct conformation is a plus and will help a horse stay sound during a long performance career, but a lot depends on the heart of the horse. My husband Bob's rope horse, Oney, for example, is really not the most correct horse, but he is an awesome rope and gymkhana horse. If you watch Oney walk, he paddles in the front and doesn't even look as though he would be capable of running, but he can easily keep up with the fastest steers.

The size of your horse does have some impact on your competitive choices. Obviously I would not ask a little horse like Bombay to be a head horse. Even though he might have the willingness to do so, it would be unfair to him. At 14.3 hands and without the bulky stature of a quarter horse, Bombay would most likely suffer negative physical effects after a time if he was asked to pull steers very often for team roping.

R.C., who is conformationally more correct than Oney, really does not like to run all that fast, but prefers to poke along at a slower rate, which is great for the novice rider who is just learning. Every horse has his place in life, just as each individual person does.

Always ride a prospective horse, or at the very least have a person come with you who is trustworthy and ride the horse. While there are many honest and hard-working horse people out there, the few that aren't honest are the ones who can get a novice hurt.

When I go with a client to look for a horse, I like to saddle the horse myself, clean the hooves, brush the horse, lead it around, and get a sense of how this horse is going to be. I watch the eye and look for signs of discomfort or annoyance. Is this horse happy to be around people or tense and uptight? Is the horse eager to please or does he have the attitude of "Oh, brother!" I once rode a horse (for a client) whom the seller had

Finding the Right Horse

When looking for a horse for a speed event such as gymkhanas, team or breakaway roping, or team penning, consider these factors.

- How much training does the horse have?

- A horse for a novice rider needs to at least have seen a barrel or steer. Better yet, take an experienced horse person with you to check your candidate out.

- Does the horse have good feet and legs? (Remember the old saying "No feet, no horse," and look for spavins or splints that may affect the horse's performance.)

- Look for a strong, well-muscled hip and a shoulder to match the strain that the horse will experience when performing these events.

- Has the horse had any illnesses or injuries in the past?

- How does the horse act away from home ground? (This is a really important question. I have seen horses that were fine when ridden on home ground, but once away from the familiar territory and/or their friends they become nut cases. While time and training may reduce this potentially dangerous behavior, you could be in for heartbreak.)

- Will the horse trailer alone and with other horses in a reasonably calm manner? If you can't trailer the horse, it's hard to compete.

- Is the horse an easy keeper?

- Undesirable behavior—such as stall weaving, pawing, cribbing, biting, kicking, rearing, bucking, or pulling back—is a no-no.

assured me was a great horse. When I asked for a lope the horse started bucking. The seller commented, "Oh, he hasn't done that in a while!"

Remember the saying "Pretty is as pretty does." I have seen some great working horses who weren't at all pretty, but who were awesome on cattle or in gymkhanas. So don't make the typical first-time buyer mistake of falling in love with a horse because of his color or his pretty head.

Since I enjoy versatility and my horses all double as lesson horses as well, they have all been trained to perform a variety of tasks, everything from cattle events to jumping and gymkhanas. Most people can't afford more than one horse, so finding one who is capable of performing a multiple events becomes important. Gymkhanas and cattle events vary in what they require of a horse, so it stands to reason that a good, all-around horse needs to be a multitalented athlete, but when I look for an all-around horse, the *first* thing I look for is a willing disposition. On the other hand, if your interest lies strictly in one discipline, like barrels or team roping, then you are shopping for a horse whose talent will make him a superstar in one particular event.

Above all, you must ask yourself whether you and the horse "click." I have seen horses who will "take care of" a novice rider. These horses seem to sense that their rider or handler means well, and despite receiving conflicting signals, these horses perform well. I have also seen horses and riders who just don't get along, and while neither horse nor rider may be totally at fault, as a team they are a disaster.

If a seller will allow it, one way to "test drive" your potential relationship with a prospective purchase is to take the horse on trial. This way you can see how the horse responds to you, out of his "normal" environment, and how you and he get along. You can also have the horse checked by your own veterinarian during this trial period. There is some risk involved when a seller allows a buyer to remove a horse from the seller's personal care and/or property. Not all sellers are willing to take

A young California gymkhana competitor correctly attired in a long-sleeve shirt, clean jeans, and safety helmet, sits her horse in a nicely balanced position. This team gives the feeling of being a "perfect match," for each other and for the discipline.

that risk, so don't assume something is wrong with a horse just because a seller may not want to let the horse go out "on trial." However, a seller should be willing to allow you to come and try a horse more than once as a normal part of the buying process.

Sometimes it takes a few months to find that particular horse who is just right for your needs (see the example of a good match in the photo below). Don't get impatient; in the long run, you and the horse you choose will be much happier for your diligence and thoroughness.

Gymkhana Events

The patterns for different gymkhana events vary from the simplest to more complicated patterns. Following is a description of some of the events found at various gymkhanas. When practicing, whether at home or in another arena, always use the correct measurements for the pattern you are working. By doing this, you and your horse become familiar with the pattern *and* the distance. It is much better to practice a pattern the way you will ride it in competition than to get to an event and have the pattern longer or shorter.

Barrel Racing

In the most common version of this event, where the pattern is run around three barrels (as shown in the diagram on the following page), you may chose either barrel to begin your run. If you take the right barrel first and turn right, then the next two barrels will be left turns. If you chose to take the first barrel and turn left, then the next two barrels will

A young California competitor and her horse make a tight, beautifully balanced turn around a barrel.

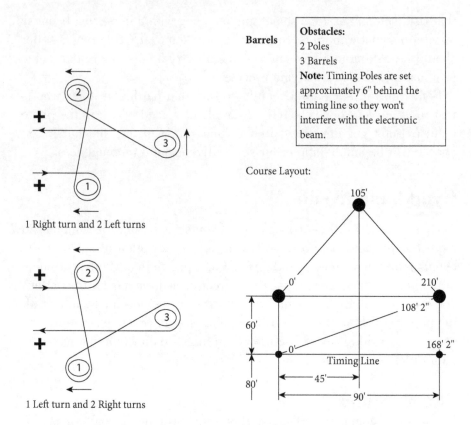

Barrels

Obstacles:
2 Poles
3 Barrels
Note: Timing Poles are set approximately 6" behind the timing line so they won't interfere with the electronic beam.

1 Right turn and 2 Left turns

1 Left turn and 2 Right turns

Course Layout:

be right turns. A smart competitor will choose the direction that gives them two turns in the direction in which their horse is supplest and can turn the tightest and fastest. You must start through the timing line and finish through the timing line. The winner is decided on time. There is a time penalty for any barrel knocked down.

Pole Bending (Washington)

Go through the timing line along either side of the poles, ride down to the last pole in the line, turn around that last pole and begin weaving through the poles. When you reach the beginning pole, turn around this pole and weave back (as shown in the diagram on the following page) toward the last pole, which you will once again turn around, then run a straight line back, on the opposite side from the one you originally started on, toward the timing line. There is a penalty for each pole knocked down and a no-time for running off course.

Pole bending.

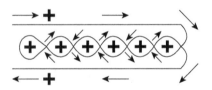

Right turn at last pole

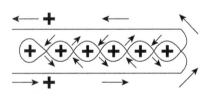

Left turn at last pole

Obstacles:
8 Poles

Note: Timing Poles are set approximately 6" behind the timing line so they won't interfere with the electronic beam.

Course Layout:

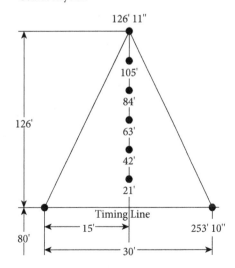

Keyhole

Go through the timing line and run into the circle of the keyhole, stop, turn in either direction, and return through the timing line. All four of the horse's feet must enter the circle. If any of the horse's hooves touch the ground on or outside any portion of the keyhole, the contestant will be disqualified.

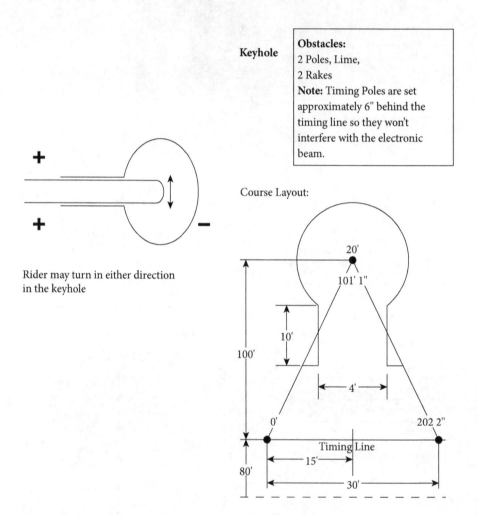

Keyhole

Obstacles:
2 Poles, Lime,
2 Rakes
Note: Timing Poles are set approximately 6" behind the timing line so they won't interfere with the electronic beam.

Rider may turn in either direction in the keyhole

Course Layout:

Quadrangle

A rider may generally start the run from either end of the course—check with the judge first. Go through the timing line, turn the first two poles of the square in the same direction, pass back through the timing line, and turn the next two poles in the opposite direction to the first two poles (two lefts and two rights, or two rights and two lefts). Then pass back through the timing line.

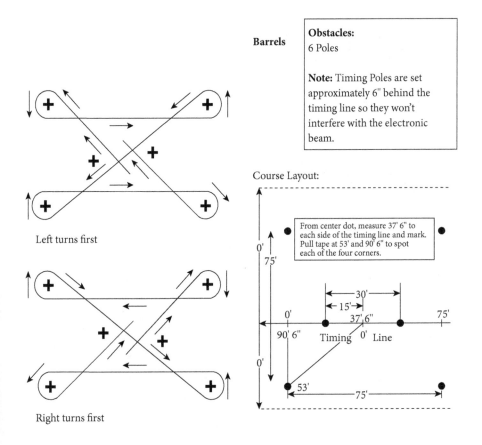

Barrels

Obstacles:
6 Poles

Note: Timing Poles are set approximately 6" behind the timing line so they won't interfere with the electronic beam.

Course Layout:

From center dot, measure 37' 6" to each side of the timing line and mark. Pull tape at 53' and 90' 6" to spot each of the four corners.

Left turns first

Right turns first

Pole Bending (California)

Go through the timing line; pass the first pole on either side. Weave through the remaining poles, turn the last pole, and weave back through the poles and pass the timing line.

Left turn at last pole

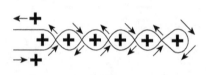

Right turn at last pole

Obstacles:
8 Poles

Note: Timing Poles are set approximately 6" behind the timing line so they won't interfere with the electronic beam.

Course Layout:

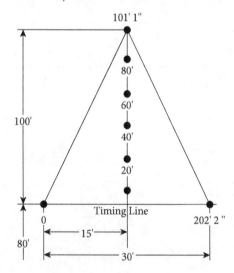

Figure-8 Flag

A rider may generally start their run from either end of the course—check with the judge first. You will be carrying a flag while you go through the timing line, go around the first barrel in either direction, and exchange the flag you are carrying for the one in the bucket on the barrel. Pass back through the timing line carrying your new flag, go around the second barrel in the opposite direction of the first barrel, and once again exchange the flag you are carrying for the one in the bucket on the barrel and pass back through the timing line. The end of the flag must be in the bucket, touching the sand. If the flag has fallen from the bucket but has not touched the ground, the rider may recover it and place it correctly in the bucket. If the flag touches the ground or the bucket is dumped, the contestant is disqualified.

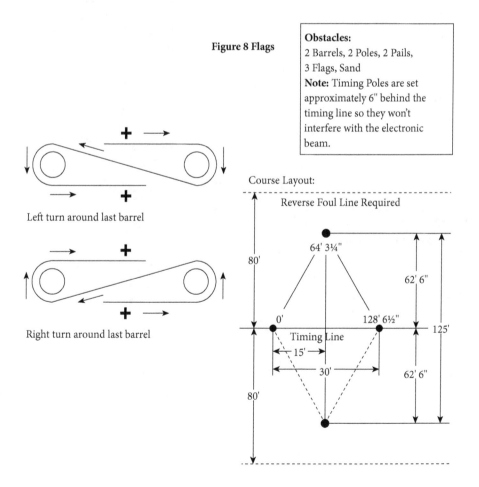

Figure 8 Flags

Obstacles:
2 Barrels, 2 Poles, 2 Pails,
3 Flags, Sand
Note: Timing Poles are set
approximately 6" behind the
timing line so they won't
interfere with the electronic
beam.

Left turn around last barrel

Right turn around last barrel

Course Layout:

Reverse Foul Line Required

64' 3¼"

80'

62' 6"

0'   128' 6½"

125'

Timing Line

15'

30'

62' 6"

80'

Hurry Scurry Competition

Two distinct competitions are available, known as Table 1 and Table 2. For both, the jumps are to be 18 inches high and 10 feet long and the jump will be approximately 4 by 4 inches and parallel to the timing line.

Start through the timing line, taking either the single jump or the double jump first (it is the rider's choice which one to begin with), around the pole, and over whichever jump remains and back through the timing line. There is a penalty for knocking down a jump.

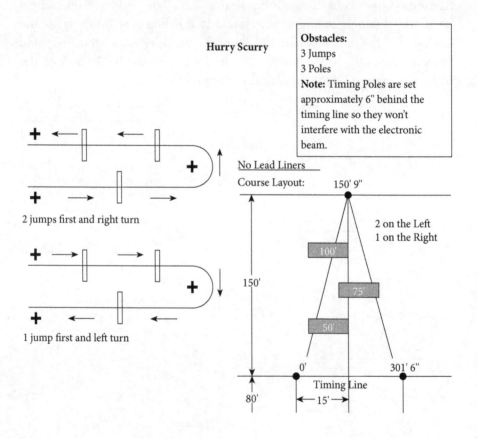

Speed Ball

Go through the timing line to the cone. Turn the cone in either direction, dropping the golf ball into the cone and go back through the timing line. A rider will be disqualified if the golf ball does not go inside the cone or if the cone is knocked over.

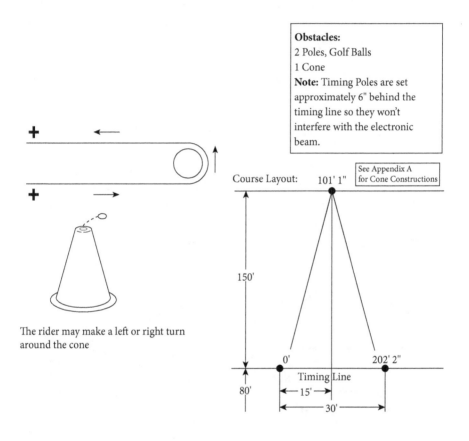

Obstacles:
2 Poles, Golf Balls
1 Cone
Note: Timing Poles are set approximately 6" behind the timing line so they won't interfere with the electronic beam.

Course Layout: 101' 1"   See Appendix A for Cone Constructions

The rider may make a left or right turn around the cone

150'

0'   202' 2"

Timing Line

80'   ←—15'—→

←————30'————→

Two-Man Ribbon Race

The contestants are handed a piece of crepe paper ribbon, 4 feet long and 2 to 4 inches wide, which they must hold in the hand that is not holding the bridle reins. Each must retain their hold on the ribbon from the timing line around the stake in either direction and back to the timing line. Dropping either end or breaking the ribbon shall result in disqualification. Riders may not link arms, hold hands, or have their horses connected in any way.

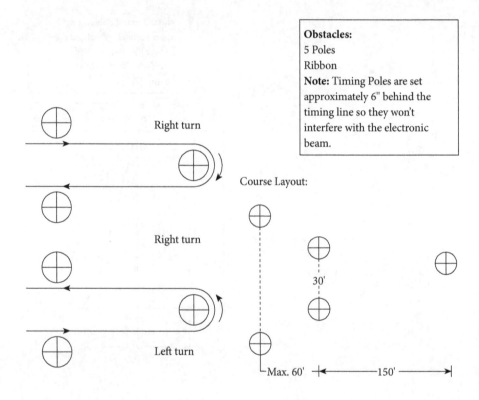

Obstacles:
5 Poles
Ribbon
Note: Timing Poles are set approximately 6" behind the timing line so they won't interfere with the electronic beam.

Right turn

Right turn

Left turn

Course Layout:

30'

Max. 60' |←————150'————→|

Big "T"

Go through the timing line, pass the first pole on either side, and weave through the next two poles. If the third pole is passed on the right side, proceed to the barrel on your left making a left turn and another left turn around the other barrel. Then weave back through the three poles to pass through the timing line.

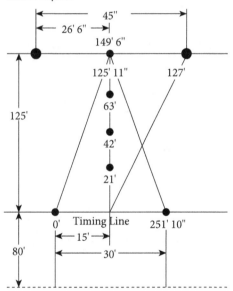

Big "T"	**Obstacles:** 5 Poles 2 Barrels **Note:** Timing Poles are set approximately 6" behind the timing line so they won't interfere with the electronic beam.

Course Layout:

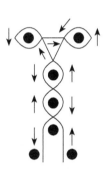

Left turn around each of the two barrels

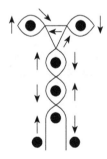

Right turn around each of the two barrels

Birangle

Go through the timing line and run to the inside of either pole. Turn the pole and run to the second pole, turning it in the same direction as the first pole. Go back through the timing line to end run.

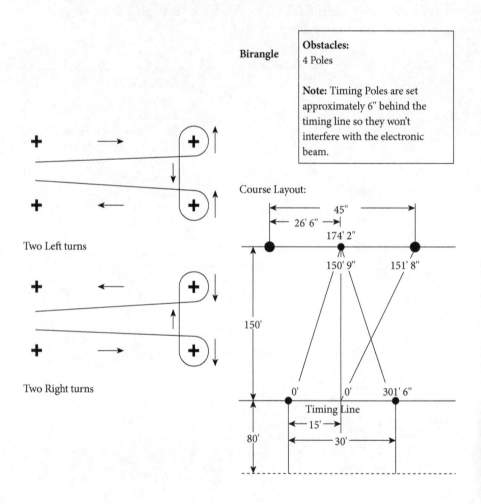

Birangle

Obstacles:
4 Poles

Note: Timing Poles are set approximately 6" behind the timing line so they won't interfere with the electronic beam.

Two Left turns

Two Right turns

Course Layout:

Speed Barrels

Go through the timing line, pass the first barrel in either side, weave through the remaining two, turning around the third barrel, weave through the barrels, and go back through the timing line.

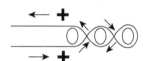

Left turn around end barrel

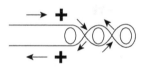

Right turn around end barrel

Obstacles:
2 Poles
3 Barrels
Note: Timing Poles are set approximately 6" behind the timing line so they won't interfere with the electronic beam.

Course Layout:

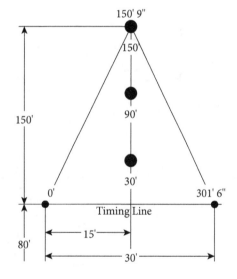

Single Stake

Ride through the timing line to the pole, going around the pole in either direction, return to the timing line. If the pole is knocked over during the run, the contestant is disqualified.

Obstacles:
3 Poles

Note: Timing Poles are set approximately 6" behind the timing line so they won't interfere with the electronic beam.

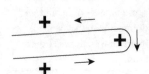

Left turn around pole

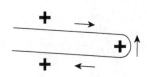

Right turn around pole

Course Layout:

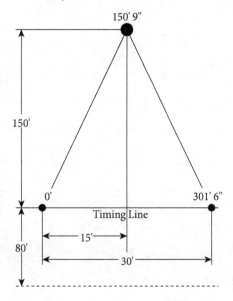

A Uniquely American Sport

Rodeo is a distillation of both America's past and the cowboy's skills, which are displayed during the various contests. The contests symbolize both who we are and where we came from. To watch cowboys and cowgirls ride in a rodeo today, one cannot help but picture the Wild West with all the turmoil, heartache, and joys those days once held.

Team Roping/Breakaway Roping

Like barrel racing, team roping (and breakaway roping, discussed in the following section) is among the most popular rodeo events today. The origin of these events is easily traced to the cowboy. The TV movie *Lonesome Dove* portrayed this portion of American history, a time of cattle, horses, and land without end. Perhaps today's contestants feel as though they are connected to those adventurous days of the old West, when driving, chasing, roping, penning, branding, and doctoring were all a part of the yearly tasks of the cowboy. Then again, perhaps they've discovered that these activities, apart from being useful skills, are just plain fun to take part in (see the photo below), just like the ranch hands of the past who turned their working skills into friendly contests on a Sunday afternoon, to see who could ride the hardest or fastest, and who could get their rope around a steer the quickest.

Breaking from the chute.

Caught!

The team roping contests of today not only reflect the technique used in the past, they also utilize skills still in use in some present-day cattle operations. In team roping there is a header, a heeler, and a steer (as shown in the photo above).

1. The *header* is in a box to the left of the steer that is in a chute and the *heeler* is in a "box" to the right of the steer.

2. The header asks for the release of the steer from the chute with a nod of his head, at which point the steer in the chute is released.

3. The steer is given a head start by virtue of a barrier.
   The barrier is a spring-loaded string device stretched across the front of the chute where the header and his horse wait while the steer is released. It is designed to ensure that all contestants

begin their competition run at the same point. If the header's horse jumps out after the steer too early, the string barrier is broken and the team incurs a ten-second penalty. Both the header and the heeler will run out after the steer once it is released from the chute, as soon as they are sure the steer has had enough time to trip the barrier release.

4. The header comes up on the steer's left side and, throwing his loop, catches the head of the steer, dallies the rope to his saddle horn, and then turns the steer to the left, pulling the steer behind him.

5. It is now the heeler's job to come in from behind, throw his loop, and catch both back feet of the steer.

6. The heeler will finish the run by stopping his horse while simultaneously dallying his rope around the saddle horn.

7. As soon as the steer is caught (see the photo on pages 184–185), the header must turn his horse and face the steer and his heeler.

8. Time is called by an arena judge, or flagger, who waits until both ropes are tight, and both header and heeler are facing the steer.

9. At this point, the flagger will lower the flag, signaling the timekeeper to stop the clock and record the team's time.

Penalties are incurred when the barrier has been broken at the start of the run (ten seconds) or if the heeler was able to rope only one hind foot (five seconds). If either the header or heeler misses the steer, the team will receive a no-time. The only legal catches for a header are around the horns, around the neck, or a half-head (a horn and neck combination).

The head rope is usually a 30-foot-long rope that can be extra-soft, soft, medium-soft, and so on. The feel of the rope is a personal choice. The heeler's rope is usually a 35-foot-long rope and can be hard, medium-hard, or extra-hard—again, it is a personal choice.

Breakaway Roping

Breakaway calf roping can be a lot of fun. Winning times are usually in the two- to three-second range, with times being recorded in the hundredths of a second. The contestant and the horse are in the heeler's side of the release chute or to the right of the calf. Also, as in team roping, there is a barrier that the contestant must be aware of. The calf is in the chute. At a nod from the contestant the calf is released, and allowing for the barrier, the contestant and the horse race after the calf. As soon as the contestant is able, they throw their loop and catch the calf around the neck, at the same instant stopping the horse and releasing the rope, which is tied to the saddle with a piece of string. When the horse stops with the calf still running, the string breaks away. The flagger then drops the flag and the time stops. A ten-second penalty will be given for breaking the barrier.

The rope usually used for breakaway roping is extra-soft to soft and is 28 to 30 feet long. Once again personal choice dictates what brand of rope and the lay and length of the rope. One helpful tip is to tie a bandana or some such lightweight visible piece of material on the rope at the breakaway point. This enables the flagging person to see the end of

Arena Footing

Arenas differ greatly in type of footing, which can range from deep sand (as shown in the photo below) to native soil to decomposed shavings and everything in between. Always check the footing in the arena you are about to compete in. Does it have slick spots; is it deeper in one section of the arena as opposed to other sections; is it rocky or clumpy; how are your horse and the other horses moving in the footing?

These are all thoughts to keep in mind and check out before your run. Adjusting your run to whatever the footing is will save injury to you and your horse.

the breakaway rope more easily, which may result in a better time. Always check the rules and regulations, since these can vary. Some events allow two loops to be used, others do not, and some have rules as to what type of string can be used to tie your rope to the saddle horn. The only "legal" catch in breakaway roping is around the calf's neck in some rodeos; other rodeos will count a loop settling over the nose of the calf if the rope breaks away on its own. All other catches or a failure to catch the calf result in a no-time.

Warming Up Your Horse

Always get to an event early with plenty of time to groom, saddle and warm up your horse. Arriving just before your first class begins makes for frayed nerves and is unfair to your horse. Your horse is an athlete and with that in mind you should prepare him properly. If you are first up

Heat of the Day

Since many gymkhanas and cattle events take place during summer months, be sure to keep your horse hydrated. When he is resting between runs, this is a great time to offer him some water. It is wise to bring your own water bucket; this one little task could save your horse from catching a disease. If your horse is finicky about water, bring water from home so a strange taste to the water doesn't make him refuse to drink all day long.

At the end of the day, when all is said and done, be sure to take care of your horse properly. Unsaddle him, brush him down, rub his legs down with some liniment, clean out his feet, wash off the sweat, and get him ready for the ride home. If the day has turned cool and you have a late run or two, be sure to use a cooler to prevent chilling and a blanket in the trailer (provided your horse is used to wearing one), to ensure he doesn't chill on the ride home.

and have arrived late, it is more than likely you will not have a solid run. Spending a proper amount of time warming up your horse will also tell you about his mind set that day.

When you clean his hooves stretch his legs and do leg circles—instruction on these stretching exercises for your equine athlete can be found in the TTEAM (Tellington Touch Equine Awareness Method) books. In the arena or warm-up area, walk, trot, and *then* canter your horse. Do *not* go racing up and down the arena, turning him this way and that. Save your speed for your runs. Have a warm-up routine that fits your horse. Some horses require a longer warm-up period than others do. Get your horse to flex, do figure-8s and pay attention to you. Addressing the needs of your horse will go a long way toward preventing or minimizing injury and/or lameness and help you and your horse to have a good run.

Gymkhanas are multiple events, so you and your horse could be standing around much of the time. Depending on the size of the gymkhana, it could last several hours to all day. Use good judgment and keep track of when you are up in the next event, use the down time to take care of your horse. Dismount and loosen the cinch. If you just sit in the saddle all day long, it is very tiring for the horse and you want him at his best for his next run. Letting him relax between runs keeps him fresh and he will do a better job for you when it comes time to perform again. Depending on the size of the gymkhana, it could be an hour between your runs, so always check and (if necessary) tighten your cinch before each run, especially if you've been waiting around for a while. Move your horse around to warm him up again. Treat him wisely and he will perform better and longer.

Training the Young Horse

When working with a young horse as a gymkhana prospect or a cattle event horse, start all work *slowly*. Yes, the ultimate goal is to have a horse who can fly with the wind around barrels or poles, or be able to catch the fastest of steers and calves, but you must establish control before you ask for speed, and your horse will need to understand what is being asked of him.

Ground Training

I always start a horse with ground training. Your horse should listen and respond in a calm manner when you are working him on the ground. I like to see a horse who really pays attention to the handler and is able to focus on the task at hand. I personally have found the TTEAM method very helpful in working with the young horse as well as with older ones. TTEAM bodywork and ground exercises are a great way to build a relationship with your horse. The bodywork not only helps the horse relax, it also helps the person doing the body work relax. A relaxed and calm horse learns much more readily than a nervous horse. This also holds true for a nervous person handling their first horse or a new horse performing at their first show or a big, important event.

In doing the ground work with the horse, I place various obstacles around, then challenge the horse by leading him over and through, asking him to focus, think, and calmly solve questions that at first might tend to cause him to panic. Wherever I have an obstacle placed, I require the horse to really look at the object and look to me for guidance. If the horse is jumping at every sound and sight, I will really focus on having him pay attention to me and on what is being expected of him by asking the horse to lower his head and really check the obstacle out.

By having the horse look at and smell the object, and seeing that I am not really upset by the presence of this strange thing, my horse can begin to relax and trust me. Once the horse is calmer and really trusting and focusing on the handler, start adding stranger obstacles to the mix. Try using a tarp or several tarps of different colors, a tree branch with leaves that rattle in the breeze, tires, ropes, water—anything one might encounter in the real world. Remember to keep it to a level the horse can handle and to advance challenges in very small increments over multiple working sessions. If the horse starts getting upset, back off and slow down. The concept of "advance and retreat" works for more things than just round pen sessions. In this way your horse will be able to learn to accept new things, look to you for guidance, and learn to "wait and see" instead of reacting by trying to "hightail it out of here."

On their own, horses in the field or in the wild are curious by nature. If the unusual doesn't attack, they will slowly stretch their neck out and approach in order to smell the foreign thing that is in their domain. Using the same approach in training is being smart. Let your horse become accustomed to the item before going on. Don't rush him!

Teaching the horse to lower his head is the best way to diffuse a potentially explosive situation and has the added benefit of short-circuiting the pull back reflex. Gymkhana and cattle event horses are continually taken to places that are not safe and sane (in the mind of the horse). There are monsters (bulls) rattling around in the release chutes; tarps and banners fluttering about; people running around on horses not always aware of where others are around them; loud music playing—the list goes on and on. By teaching your horse to lower his head, either from a light pull and release on the halter/bridle or a touch on the horse's neck, you are teaching him to relax and breathe. When a horse is startled or scared, he throws his head up, and also holds his breath, often releasing it in an explosive snort, which further frightens him. When teaching the horse to lower his head, be consistent; every time it goes up, ask for it to come back down. I'm not talking about having the horse put his nose on the ground, I just want him to be able to see what is going on around him, with his head at or a little lower than wither level, where he can still look around and view the sights (which is what I want him to do), without getting upset.

I also want to be able to move any part of the horse around at the slightest suggestion in *controlled movement*, which means not having the horse fling his hind end around because I stepped toward it, but having the horse respond a step at a time. What's the difference? It's the contrast between ballroom dancing and slam dancing. If I take one step toward the horse's hindquarters, I want the horse to take that step with me. If I keep stepping toward the hindquarters, I want the horse to mimic my movement. I am looking for a rhythm in our relationship on the ground as well as in the saddle. I am also asking him to step over correctly, which is why I am looking for controlled movement.

Once a horse is leading safely and focusing on me, I start taking him to various gymkhana, rodeo, or show events. In order to get him accustomed to all the commotion that is part of these events—plastic bottles being tossed into trash cans, kids running around, flags and banners waving, and so on—I let him stand around for part of the day watching the activities, walk him past the loud speaker, and continue working with him on the ground. Doing this will give your horse an invaluable education, which in turn will keep you and your horse much safer when you get to the point of riding him both at home and at a competition. Much of the training will be done at home, but it is always different for the horse when he is in an unknown place with numerous strange horses walking about. The more attention you put on the little things with a young horse, the better suited your horse will be for *any* activity.

Ground driving the young horse is a helpful tool in teaching and strengthening him before he is ridden. Introduce the equipment you will be using to ground drive using the same approach we have just discussed. Whether you use a surcingle or a saddle, let the horse become familiar with that piece of equipment before placing it on his body. The horse also needs to learn to accept ropes behind and around his legs. Using a calf rope or a very soft rope, start the process by stroking the horse all over with the rope. Then quietly toss the rope around the horse, working up to swinging the rope with the ultimate goal of being able to rope any body part without frightening the horse. In the end, the horse should stand quietly with a rope around his legs, tail, head, or rump. Not only does this technique ensure that once ground driving is started the horse will be unafraid of the ropes around and behind him, but it is also useful in starting a rope horse or a calf-roping horse.

Using a Lindell or a side pull (bitless bridle), attach one rope on one side only, using a quick-release knot in case the horse becomes anxious. Having someone lead the horse, take the rope first out to the side, then slowly bring the rope toward the rear of the horse. Be sure to give yourself plenty of room in case the horse kicks. If you have taken the time and done all the preliminary desensitizing work, kicking should not be a problem. Gently stroke the horse with the rope, letting him feel the rope along his side and legs. A helper should be holding and, from the front, stroking the horse with a wand (crop) and asking the horse to lower his head if he raises it. Once the horse is relaxed about having you and the rope behind him, ask the person leading the horse to walk him out a few steps and whoa. If the horse is relaxed, have the leader turn the horse in a circle in each direction so the horse feels the rope on his legs. Following this procedure, do the same on the other side. Now that the horse is comfortable with the rope on both sides, attach a driving line on each side to the Lindell. Still using a person to lead the horse, have the horse turn in circles in both directions, walking a straight line, stopping, and backing. Reinforce the whoa. Once the person in front is no longer there, the horse will need to respond to the signal given through the driving lines and to the voice command of whoa, no matter what. As you progress, more of the signals must come from the person driving the horse, with the leader reinforcing the signals as necessary. When the horse is listening and is responsive to the driver's signals consistently, it's time to solo.

Starting with a rectangular pattern of cones on the ground (see the figure on this page), drive your horse in straight lines, circles, and serpentines. Be creative; try setting ground poles at various points to encourage the horse to pick up his feet, or place barrels in the pattern. This method is great for providing the horse with many of the elements he is going to need once you start riding him. Ground driving gets the horse used to things touching him around his haunches and rear legs and having someone behind him, which is helpful no matter what your discipline.

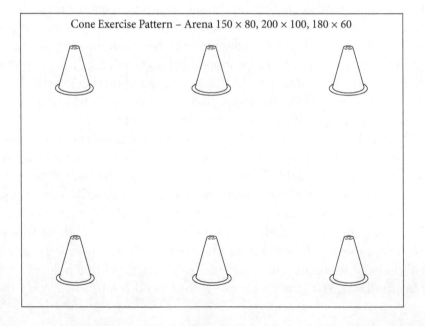

Cone Exercise Pattern – Arena 150 × 80, 200 × 100, 180 × 60

On-the-Horse Training

Once the horse is responding quietly and consistently to being ground driven through obstacles, then he is ready for the next step, being ridden. Depending on the horse, I will sometimes use the Lindell alone or with a snaffle bit. If using a snaffle bit, get the horse used to it during the ground driving sessions by allowing him to carry it in his mouth without attaching any reins. Be sure the bit fits correctly and comfortably. There are many types of bits, but the snaffle is generally considered the bit of choice to start a horse. However, it isn't quite that easy because there are many different types of snaffles, especially mouthpieces. Remember that the horse is still young, so start off slowly.

Training takes time, and the more time you spend making sure you have a solid horse, the better you and your horse will perform in the long run. Also remember that all work and no play makes for an unhappy horse. In order to give your horse a break in his daily routine, along with the arena work, take him out on a trail ride and work him on cattle.

If the walk isn't crisp and controlled, none of the other gaits will be, so start your training with a simple walk (as shown in the photo on the following page), and work to have your horse really walk out like he means business. I don't mean having him walk out with his head up and short choppy movements. I am looking for a well-rounded horse with smooth and easy movements. If you find your horse tends to drag his feet, use ground poles to encourage him to pick up his feet and reach. Repeatedly have him move out crisply, then slow him down to a very slow walk; switch back and forth between the faster walk and slower walk, asking for whoas in between. This encourages the engine (rear

Advance Slowly

Before you start your horse on barrels, poles, or cattle events, he should be well schooled in these movements: turning properly, lead changes, and rollbacks. Having the horse respond to your cues as opposed to reacting to a pattern or just running after cattle is extremely important, since this will allow you to continue to polish his performance until you are in the winners' circle consistently. The walk is just as important as the trot or the canter.

Walking a young horse through the pole pattern, slowly and calmly.

end) of the horse to engage. As the horse progresses in his training, this same exercise can be used at the trot and canter as well.

Now return to your rectangular pattern of cones, since the horse is already familiar with these, and start riding the horse in the same patterns you introduced during driving: circles, serpentines, straight lines, halts, and so on. The more the horse learns—bending, balancing, answering the rider's aids promptly and calmly—the better he will respond in any situation.

When your horse is handling all of these basic exercises well, it is time to move him to the next level by teaching him how to two track and do rollbacks and flying lead changes. As you do this, you will also be refining his responses, precision, and timing while teaching him to respond to your leg and weight cues, leaving the influence of the bit for polishing his performance. Your reward will be that you not only create a great riding horse but will also improve your winning ratio.

A young horse does not have the balance of an older, more well-trained horse. With this in mind, begin his training with large circles and decrease the size of the circles as he becomes balanced. As he improves on his circles, have him trot/canter a large circle, spiral down to a smaller circle, then spiral back up to the larger circle. Keep the beat of the walk/trot/canter even and smooth. If the horse has a tendency to rush the circle at any gait, address that problem before going on. If he is rushing through circles in training, you can be sure he will do the same in competition. When a horse rushes the circle or gets faster, open your inside rein away from his neck and ask your horse to flex in the direction of the circle. Use your inside leg to create bend in his ribs.

Rushing is usually a sign the horse is leaning on the circle rather than bending himself to travel an arcing line. When he responds to the inside rein pressure and *gives* his head and neck to the inside, check his forward progress lightly with the outside rein, asking him to balance himself more over his hind feet and slow or collect his gait. Checking with the outside rein is a give and release action. Do not apply a continuous hold, as it will teach your horse to lean against the bit, rather than rebalancing himself, in response to pressure. As soon as the horse responds, release or lighten your aides to indicate to him that his response has been correct.

If the horse is lazy and tends to slow down in the circle, use a strong inside leg to get him to stride up under himself with his inside hind leg, lifting himself up and moving his balance more toward the outside. If he still isn't responsive and moving forward crisply, tap him on the rump with a rein or riding crop.

Be sure to take time for training the whoa. The horse who anticipates what is going on without listening is a horse who is out of control. To be sure the horse is responding to you, stop him at different intervals in the pattern while training him. Before coming to a turn, have the horse stop, then ask him to make the pattern turn. This exercise accomplishes two things: you are directing the dance, and it teaches the horse to balance himself before each turn. You want to be sure that by the time you are ready to go to a gymkhana or cattle event, the horse will stop when you make the end run or are chasing down a steer. It's no fun having a horse who is galloping across the time line out of control with you wondering whether he will he stop at the fence.

One other factor that is too often overlooked is whether the horse stands quietly when being mounted and dismounted. A horse who is walking off as the rider is getting on is not paying attention. Each time you mount your horse, make sure he is standing quietly. Give him a moment to just stand there with you on him, then walk him off. Do not get on and immediately walk the horse off, especially with a young horse. If the horse moves off as you are mounting, once you are securely in the saddle, move him around in small circles, ask him to stand, then dismount and remount until he accepts your actions without trying to depart prematurely. When the horse does stand quietly while being mounted, just let him dwell for a moment or two.

Once you have started work on various gymkhana patterns with your horse, *do not* run him through the patterns over and over again. It is best to keep the speed runs for when they are needed in competitions.

A rider schooling a horse in the bending class shows a nicely balanced, slow lope during a competition.

At home, school your horse at walk, trot or jog, or lope only. For the young horse, work him for a short time on a pattern or two, and then do something fun for the horse. Go for a stroll with him out in the pasture or out on trail. By not overworking him, you will keep him interested in the pattern work. Each horse is different, as are people, and you need to be aware of your horse's mental attitude as well has his physical condition. Taking your horse's frame of mind into consideration when selecting the day's work will go a long way toward preventing him from getting sour on working gymkhana patterns, and will ensure he is both fresh and a willing partner when you do go to a competition.

Training for Events with Cattle

Start by placing a slow steer in a round pen and just have the horse follow the steer around. Once the horse gets the idea, "Hey, I'm moving this steer this way and that," you will find most horses will really start to enjoy it. Have the horse move the steer in one direction and ask for a whoa. Then swing wide of the steer and move the steer in the opposite direction. By starting in a slower and more controlled environment, the horse has a chance to assimilate all the information, the turns, the whoas, and so on. Once again, be sure to reinforce your whoa response during this phase of training.

Don't continually chase the steer around and around in one direction. This is pointless, not only in training but to the horse as well. Keeping the horse interested in what is going to come next will in turn keep the horse listening to what is being asked of him. When the horse is responding in a consistent way, it is time to take him out into the larger arena. If you are training your horse in order to be able to rope off of him, the next step is to ask him to just stand in the box with cattle in the chute. If this proves to be too much for him, ask him to stand in the roping box without the steers in the chute. By building slowly one block after another, your horse will be able to stand in the roping box without moving until he is asked, even if a steer is released. Before you "break" your horse from a chute, make sure to first walk, then trot them out of the chute, following a steer that has just been released.

I also like to teach my rope horses to drag a barrel, a pole, or some other lightweight object before I rope a steer. Be sure the horse is okay with swinging the rope with you mounted. Dangle the rope around the horse's head, legs, and butt to ensure that he is comfortable with having the rope move around with a rider on top. Then swing the rope, releasing it as though you were trying to catch a steer, and drag it back toward the horse. Remember to keep the reins steady while you do this. Don't inadvertently move the reins around while swinging the rope or coiling the rope back up. See the photos on this page for rear cinch adjustments you need to make when it comes time to actually rope a steer.

A rear cinch adjusted for normal riding.

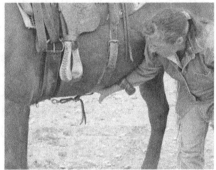

When roping, the rear cinch must be adjusted much more snugly in order to prevent the pressure on the rope from causing the front edge of the bars of the saddle to dig into your horse's shoulder and back.

Now that the horse is at ease with all the above, swing the rope and catch a barrel or pole. Ask the horse to back a step or two, reassuring him that the caught object is not coming to get him, then turn the horse and drag the object a few feet and have him face it again. Repeat this until the horse is responding calmly, at which time you can walk and trot the horse in a wide circle around the arena so he feels the weight of the object and the rope against his flank. Another word of caution: dally the rope (that is, wrap it around with one turn) to the saddle horn; *do not* tie it! To dally a rope around your saddle horn properly, wrap your rope counter clockwise and always keep your thumb up.

When you do make your first run after a steer, it is best to do so on slow-to medium-running cattle. At this point, don't rope; follow the steer so your horse can begin to understand that when you ask him to run, you want him to follow the steer. Once this understanding is ascertained, then follow a steer and rope it, but don't turn it off; just stop the steer. I like to use what is called a "breakaway hondo," which is a rope with a loop through which the rope goes; when the weight of the steer is felt, it will snap open and free the steer. This way the horse new to roping can feel a small jerk when you dally, but not the full impact of a steer hitting the end of the rope. Break the job down into individual steps to make it easy for your horse to learn any new job. If you take the time to bring a horse along slowly, you will find that in the long run, his performance will be more consistent. Keep in mind that if the horse has already been schooled in turning and stopping and ground driving, he should be used to ropes swinging around him and touching him.

My husband, Bob, and I raised longhorn cattle, so we had access to roping stock and practiced roping every Tuesday and Thursday. One roper was trying to bring a four-year-old colt along and was having trouble getting the young horse to walk into the roping box. It got to the point where the horse would set up and spin away from the roper's box before getting near it and the rider would lean forward, look at the horse, and try to force him to step forward. The whole situation was getting progressively worse with each attempt. When the roper finally asked for help, I was more than willing to step in. I had the rider dismount, then I took the horse on a lead rope and walked him around the arena, asking him to relax and walk quietly with his head down. Once I felt the horse was listening to me, I walked him into the roper's box, turned, and walked out.

After several times the horse was visibly starting to relax about being near the box, and I asked him to walk in, turn around, and stand for just a moment and then walk out quietly. With each step I reinforced that the horse could lower his head and relax. I would do the TTEAM mouth work to get him to lick and chew—a tension-releasing response that helped tremendously. With each step the horse was more responsive in lowering his head and listening to what was being asked of him. Then we placed a steer in the release chute and I asked him to walk into the roping box. As we walked in I pointed out that there was now a steer in the release chute and all was well.

The next step was to have the horse walk into the roping box, turn around, and stand quietly while the steer was released. The horse was now more relaxed and paying attention to what was happening and no longer just reacting to the scary prospect of standing in that frightening roper's box. Now it was time for the roper to get back on. With the rider in the saddle, I led them both into the roper's box. I explained to the roper that by leaning forward and looking at the horse, he was actually giving the horse an out. I asked the roper to keep his seat in the saddle, sit up straight, and look where he wanted the horse to go. I have to say this guy was a real trooper; not many cowboys would allow a woman to lead them around on their horse, but he was willing. I led them in and out several times and finally asked for a steer to be released while I stood in the box with the rider and horse. By the end of the session the roper was able to ride his horse unassisted into the roper's box and his horse would stand quietly while a steer was released. By breaking down all the parts for the horse and getting him to relax, the horse learned how to be confident rather than scared.

Taking a young horse to a small local competition is the best way to school him. This doesn't mean pushing the horse to the max; just get him out there to familiarize him with a different arena. I may just trot through a pattern and take it easy on him. If the horse is very nervous, you might even just work in the warm-up arena and sit on the sidelines to allow him to relax and just hang out for the day. Then as the season progresses and the horse gets more and more comfortable with each gymkhana, I will start upping the ante, increasing our speed, and asking for sharper turns and a quicker end run. The horse will tell me if there are any problems and what needs to be addressed. If he starts getting nervous about entering the arena, I will take the time to calm him, and return to quietly trotting him through a course. At this point I am not concerned about where we place, my only concern is creating a horse who is responsive, yet calm about performing.

Small Steps

One of the best pieces of advice about training a horse I ever received was that if a horse isn't getting what you're showing him, break down the task even further. For example, if I want a young horse to back several feet, I will not ask him the first time to back that far, I will ask for only one step backward. If that one backward step seems complicated for the horse, I will ask for one foot to move back, then the corresponding foot to move, and so on. I increase my requests for the number of steps slowly: two, three, four, five. If I asked the horse to back ten feet on the first try, he would most likely rebel. But by breaking it down into a simpler action, one step at a time, or even one foot at a time, the horse will be able to respond more easily, which in turn keeps him more relaxed, which in turn makes him easier to train.

If your horse refuses to enter an arena, that could be a sign that you have been pushing him too hard. I like to enter the arena quietly and exit quietly. At a competition I will always stop my horse completely before leaving the arena, wait for him to settle, and walk out quietly. The horse may have an energetic quality on entering and exiting the arena, but once again, it needs to be controlled energy. The horse runs when asked, turns properly when asked, and stops when asked. Keyhole is one of the events that really shows where the horse is lacking. I've seen many a rider and horse run into the keyhole pattern, only to blow through the end because they were not able to stop their horse. The horse just kept on running. In the pole-bending pattern, the horse must be listening and responsive or he will just blow through the poles with the rider jerking on the bit to get the horse through. One of my horses, R.C., isn't the quickest horse, but he does well in the pole bending because he is fluid, smooth, and consistent.

A confident and relaxed horse performs better and learns better. Be sure to let your horse know when he does well. Even if the run isn't perfect—not all runs are—give him a kind word or a pat. Just as people respond to, "Hey, you did a good job," so do horses, and it is important to let them know when they get it right, or at least acknowledge that they tried to do their best. If you hit a day when nothing goes right, keep your training work simple. Go to something the horse is comfortable with and you know will perform well, then call it a day and put him away on a positive note. You want him returning to his pasture or stall remembering it was at least okay, if not actually fun to have been working with you. Of course, if inadequate performance or loss of focus or attention is a continuing problem during training, your horse could be having physical problems, or the problem may somehow be related to the training methods.

All of this can be applied in retraining the older horse as well. As their name implies, speed events, whether gymkhana or cattle events, are fast paced. The fast starts, hard turns, and quick stops are physically demanding. The well-trained horse who is balanced and fluid is going to be able to handle the stress and strain these events pose. Yet even a well-trained horse may be subject to the inherent stimulation of quick bursts of fast running. As trainers, we need to remember that in nature, the horse would mostly use these intense bursts of speed to outrun a predator and his adrenaline is appropriately high in such a case. Just because we've called upon the behavior in a controlled environment doesn't mean the horse's adrenaline won't kick in. In fact, most horses have to learn to "turn on the juice" without getting hyped out of their minds. Part of your job as your horse's trainer and partner is going to be to let him know that he can access his speed on request, without acting like there is a bear about to eat him alive.

Training Exercises

Many riders train their own horses for speed games; in fact, that's part of the attraction of the discipline. If you'd like to do likewise, the following training exercises help you prepare your horse to do his best during competition. Each exercise not only focuses on improving the responsiveness of your horse, but also helps prepare his body for the physical effort you will ask him to make (at faster speeds) when you are actually competing. Each exercise is important and each is explained.

Spiraling Circles
Beneficial for: Conditioning the horse to move in balance, in small circles.

Execute by: Starting off with a large circle, spiral down to a smaller circle, maintaining the regularity of the gait you are in (don't allow the horse to slow or quicken his pace). To the right, maintain right bend using inside leg and rein; weight your inside seat bone; open the inside (right) rein slightly. Give your horse's outside shoulder support by keeping your left rein against his neck, but be sure *not* to cross the outside rein over the neck; push with your outside (left) leg slightly ahead of or at the cinch. Remember, go only as far as the horse is able to stay balanced and relaxed and maintain an even cadence. To spiral out, keep your horse in a right bend and use more inside leg. Use your outside (left) rein to straighten your horse *slightly* toward the larger circle. Keep the left leg passive.

Start practicing spiraling circles at a walk, and as the horse becomes balanced and understands what is being asked of him, step up to the trot and finally a lope.

Both gymkhana events and working cattle require a horse to maintain his balance in sharp turns and circles.

Caution: Don't *lean* (drop one of your shoulders closer to the ground than the other one, like an airplane dipping its wing) as you ride through the exercise with your horse.

Two Tracking

Beneficial for: Gaining independent, lateral control of the horse's hindquarters. This exercise (and your horse's ability to respond promptly) comes in handy when running gymkhana patterns such as pole bending or barrel racing, should a horse come too close to the pattern object.

Execute by: Start with a balanced, forward walk; after several strides (going to the right), place the left leg slightly behind the cinch, asking your horse to displace his haunches to the right as he continues to move forward. Your left rein should be used only to encourage just a little flexion of your horse's nose to the left. The right rein prevents the horse from falling through his right shoulder or from running forward from the pressure of your left leg; instead, he should yield his quarter to the right. Your right leg will remain passive and only come into play if the horse tries to move his quarters too far to the right away from your left leg signal.

Ride a straight line for several strides or take a short attention break. Then, reversing the aides, ask your horse to displace his haunches laterally to the left. Once the horse is responding to lateral movement from your riding aides, this exercise can be done at a trot and a lope.

Caution: Do not overuse your flexing rein (the rein on the same side as the leg you are using to move his quarters). Be sure to keep your horse moving forward during the exercise. Should the horse lose forward motion during the exercise, ride straight ahead using strong forward driving aids, then resume the exercise. Ask for only a few steps to begin.

Rollbacks

Beneficial for: Keyhole and working cattle. In order for your horse to accomplish a correct rollback, he must learn how to engage his hind feet under his body and balance himself on his hindquarters. It is really cool when you can rollback and race out of the keyhole pattern, or you have to catch a steer that just changed directions on you.

Execute by: Riding your horse down the long side of the arena, ask for lateral movement away from the fence (two-track) as you approach the middle. Check the horse so he shifts his weight to the hindquarters, weight your left (side toward the fence) seat bone, open the left rein for slight flexion to the left, then step into your left stirrup while your right rein guides the front end around. Use your right leg forward of the cinch to encourage the horse to bring his shoulders around more quickly. As soon as your horse is facing the opposite direction, ask for forward motion. Practice at a walk and a trot before going on to the lope.

Once the horse is responding nicely to the above exercise, ride the horse in a circle to the right; ask for a whoa, and immediately ask for a 180-degree turn to the left. Again, as soon as the horse has turned, ask for forward motion and ride the circle (now going to the left) and follow the same procedure.

Caution: Take care not to overflex your horse when teaching him the turn. If he bends his neck too much, you will loose his hindquarters in the opposite direction. The pivot foot (left foot in this example) should be firmly planted as the horse pivots around.

Flying Lead Changes

Beneficial for: Barrels, pole bending, cattle work, the list is endless!

Execute by: Ask the horse for a canter on the right lead, canter down the long side of the arena, and canter both corners. On the opposite long side toward the middle, cut across the arena, making sure your horse is moving in a straight line. After a couple of straight strides, flex your horse slightly to the left (a new direction), increase your pace slightly as you head into the opposite corner, place your right leg behind cinch, and at the point of suspension, push your horse's haunches in the new direction (left), stepping into the lead stirrup as you do. Your horse should seek to rebalance himself for the corner by executing a flying lead change.

Caution: Before you teach your horse flying lead changes, he should be able to take either lead from a trot.

The Whoa

Beneficial for: As I have stated previously, being able to stop your horse is just as important as getting him to go forward. Whoa means *stop*, period. This means you must be conscious of what you are saying to your horse. If your horse is going too fast and you want him to slow down a bit, don't say "whoa," but use a word like "easy." If you say "whoa" and then let him continue to move, or fail to enforce the command completely, you are training him to ignore the command. When it is most important, you will not have this essential safety tool.

Execute by: If you say "whoa," whether you "pick up" or tighten the reins, sit deeply and use your seat and back, lean back with your shoulders, or push on your stirrups, if he does not stop and stand still, restate or reapply the command (series of aids) again, perhaps a little more firmly. If the horse still isn't responsive, pick up your inside rein in a short hold, bending his neck, and bring the horse's nose to your knee, at the same time using your leg on the same side to disengage or "push" his hindquarters away from the direction in which you are circling him. This, in effect, serves to cut off the power to his drive train.

When your horse does stop, give a release on the rein and tell him "good boy." If you take the time to teach your horse a true "whoa," where he plants his feet and grows roots until you again signal him to move forward, both your life and his will be much safer and saner, especially when you go to competitions.

Once again, start with walking and trotting, and as the horse progresses in his training and willingness to obey the "whoa," only then should you move to the canter. Be sure you are sitting down in your saddle when you are asking your horse to stop. Use as little rein pressure as possible.

Caution: Do not pull back on your reins continuously, "hanging" on them; rather, when you use them in coordination with your other aids signaling for a halt, use a light, rhythmic squeezing or "bump" and release (of tension), increasing with intensity until the horse responds. Once the horse has stopped, all pressure on the reins should immediately be released.

A Word of Advice

Novice riders should not be put on a green horse or a horse who is too powerful. Both of these situations are guaranteed to lead to injuries sooner or later, not only for the rider but for the horse and possibly for others as well.

It Takes Only a Second

I had one client whose child was taking lessons with me. During one lesson, her mother asked me a question and I briefly took my attention off her daughter to answer her. I turned back to the child just in time to see her bend over and walk under the horse's belly to clean the feet on the other side. Once my heart started beating again, I explained to both the parent and the child what a bad idea that was and why. Luckily the horse she was working with was an older, quiet, sensible horse, who stood patiently as that young child ventured into and out of a potentially life-threatening situation.

For the young child or older adult who has had little or no experience with horses, look for the seasoned horse who not only knows the game but is also "laid back" about performing. Parents who get a young horse for their young child are asking for trouble. It is like asking two first graders to teach each other English and math —neither knows how to spell or add and subtract, so it doesn't work. The horse gets frustrated and unruly, the child either becomes angry or scared, and both have lost an opportunity to find the reward that is in the experience.

This also holds true for the novice adult rider. If you have not had much experience with horses, find someone who is trustworthy and knowledgeable who can help you find a horse to match your skill level. Taking lessons with a certified instructor *before* you buy is a great way to increase your skill and learn more about horses and competition.

Older horses may require a little extra care, but they have much to offer and can be reliable and safe mounts, especially to learn on.

A big fear of the novice rider (especially the adult novice) is going fast. This fear can discourage a rider from entering a gymkhana. I encourage people, whether adult or child, to enter these events just for fun. You do not have to run full out if you are just learning how to ride. Walk or trot the pattern, and don't worry about what other people think. Go only as fast as you are comfortable going. If you have a desire to join in and be a part of a gymkhana, do so. I have found that as time goes on, the novice rider (like the one in the top photo on the following page) gains confidence in their horse and their ability to ride, and with that they start increasing speed. This approach produces a team that will eventually excel. Experience is a great confidence booster.

Age has little to do with one's ability to enjoy gymkhana events.

A Few Words on Equipment

I prefer a well-built leather saddle (see the photo below), which is more costly than a synthetic saddle but in the long run seems to fit a horse better and last longer. Since I rope as well as compete in gymkhanas, I use a Crates saddle, which is a woman's ranch saddle that is reasonably lightweight yet sturdy enough for roping. A roping saddle needs to have a reinforced horn for dallying.

The most important factor in buying a saddle is whether it fits your horse properly. You might find you want to consult with a knowledgeable professional on saddle fit before you spend your money. Most tack stores will let you take a saddle to try the fit, but unless you know how to check a saddle for fit, you may still end up buying the wrong equipment. Don't assume tack store clerks are knowledgeable about saddle fit. Ask for specifics. Just because they have been riding for twenty years doesn't guarantee they have the professional expertise to help you fit a saddle to

A working western saddle.

Tips to Keep in Mind

One factor that can make or break a solid run is where you place yourself when you start and how straight a line you make your end run. Zigzag or unnecessary diagonal lines will cost you time.

As you near the timing line, do not slow down until you have crossed it. Small arenas with less space after the timing line require a prompt response to your whoa command. Remember that speed plus control equals winning.

Look at the path you want your horse to take, not directly at the obstacle you are going toward.

A common misconception is that if a horse isn't stopping, you should put a harsher bit on him. That myth has ruined many good horses.

Prior to the beginning of each gymkhana, the basic principles are to read and listen, since rules may vary from place to place.

Make sure you don't get eliminated simply because you are not wearing the appropriate attire.

When roping, your back cinch should be tight so that when the steer hits the end of the rope, the back of the saddle will not pop up.

A breast collar should also be used to help stabilize the saddle when a steer or a calf is roped. This applies to both the header and the heeler.

When practicing roping on the ground, do not step forward when throwing the rope to make your catch. Stand on the ground as though you were on a horse and holding the reins.

Practice keeping your rein hand steady so you are not inadvertently asking the horse to turn left when you make a throw.

Make a pretend dally each time you throw your rope. By consistently practicing as though you were on a horse, your body will remember what to do once you *are* roping on a horse.

your horse. A horse with a sore back won't perform his best and may also develop dangerous training or behavior problems, like bucking or rearing. Don't assume that simply adding an extra saddle pad or blanket will improve the fit of a saddle that doesn't fit in the first place.

Protecting your horse's legs is important. I use leg protection (see the top photo on the following page) on all of my horses. My personal choice

It's a good idea to use leg protection on your competitive horse.

is the "Professional's Choice" boot. These boots last a long time, stay on the horse in all types of arena footing, and do not allow a lot of dirt between the boot and the horse's skin.

There are so many styles and types of bits (see the photo below) that it would take a separate book to cover them all. Horses are like people in their individual differences, so the same bit is not going to be comfortable for every horse.

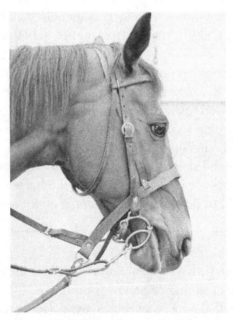

This Sharon Camarillo Sweet 6 bit is an example of an elevator bit. This barrel racer also wears the often-seen "standing martingale."

Each horse's mouth is going to vary somewhat and this is something to keep in mind when choosing a bit. If you want to save yourself a lot of training and performance headaches, remember that a harsher bit isn't the answer to solving a problem you are having with a horse.

As far as saddle pads go, I find a wool or a wool-blend saddle blanket with a well-made pad works best for me. My horse Bombay is allergic to synthetic blankets, so I tend to stick to a natural fiber like wool. For roping you want a thick pad that has a lot of cushion. This helps protect your horse's back from the jerks they tend to get whether you are team roping or breakaway roping.

Maintenance is the key in keeping tack both safe and looking good. Check all your tack at least once a month. Is the near and offside latigo in good shape? I once watched as a friend's latigo broke just as he caught a steer. As the saddle, rider, and pads started slipping off, you could see him mouthing, "Oh ?!#&!" It was quite comical to watch and ended without injury, but it could have been a disaster. It was a good reminder to check *everything* to avoid what could be a senseless accident.

Mopping up a near wreck, a helper stoops to pick up this horse's saddle blankets that fell off when the saddle, which wasn't securely cinched up, slipped. Fortunately no one was injured.

Chapter 9

Team Penning

Three on Three

In this event, thirty head of cattle are bunched at the far end of the arena. At the other end of the arena is a pen in which cattle, wearing the numbers assigned to the team's go-around, are to be "penned," or contained. See the figure on the following page.

Cattle are usually marked with numbers on their backs or have colored chains around their necks. A "team" of three riders enters the arena. One or more of the riders will cross the halfway mark in the arena, moving toward the cattle. When that line is crossed, the announcer will give the riders a number or color. If the number is 5, for example, the three riders must find the three head of cattle that carry the number 5 and get them into the pen. The riders may not allow more than four head of cattle across the halfway line on the pen end of the arena. If five or more cross the halfway line, the team is automatically and immediately disqualified. The riders may pen one to three of the correctly numbered cattle and call for a time. When time is called, all other cattle must be on the far side (away from the pen) of the halfway line. Calling for a time when a wrong-numbered or -colored cow is either in the pen or on the pen side of the halfway line is also cause for disqualification.

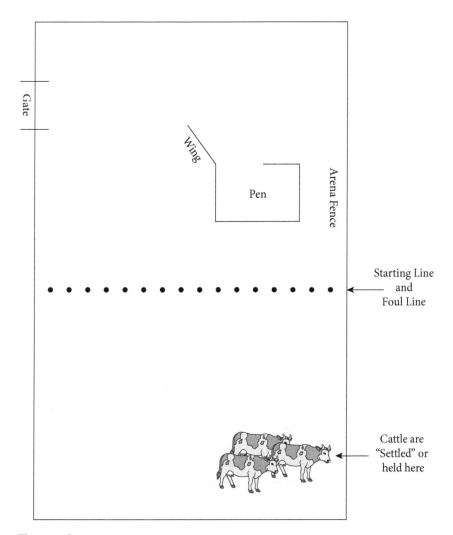

Three on three.

When (only) the correct cattle are in the pen, one rider of the team rides into the open gate of the pen so just the horse's head and neck are inside the gate, then raises one hand in the air (as shown in the top photo on the following page).

If the cattle are pushed too hard, or touched in any way by rider or horse, the judge may disqualify the team. The time limit for three on three is two and a half minutes. The team with the quickest time and most cattle penned win the round.

One rider and horse going into the open gate.

The ideal situation is to be able to push the correct cattle down along the arena fence line on the hole side of the pen. This way the three riders can work together to guide the cattle toward the pen. Once the cattle are headed in the proper direction, the rider behind the cattle will be able to cover the "hole" to prevent the cattle from turning around and rejoining their bovine friends left behind (as shown in the bottom photos on this page). Meanwhile, the other two riders go to the "wing" portion of the pen and work together to encourage or move the three cows into the pen.

One team member blocks the "hole" while the other team member attempts to push the cow into the pen.

Somehow I don't think this is how it's supposed to work, Lightning!

The longer a team works and practices together, the more they develop a rhythm and are able to read each other, knowing almost intuitively where the cattle and their teammates will go. That type of teamwork greatly increases the potential of winning.

Two on One

This event has ten head of cattle "settled" at the far end of the arena and teams of two riders. All the same rules apply as in three on three, except the two on one team only needs to sort and move one cow out of the bunch and into the pen at the far end of the arena (see the photo series on the two following pages). This team may not have more than two head of cattle across the halfway line, and their time limit is one and a half minutes.

A novice father-daughter team of two make their way quietly toward the cattle.

Upon arriving at the cattle, the appropriately numbered cow is carefully and quietly selected and separated from the rest of the herd.

Dad does the speed work, moving the correctly numbered cow up the arena toward the pen as quickly as possible.

With the cow in place, moving toward the pen, the daughter guards the hole, while Dad blocks the steer's attempted retreat back the way he came. He also puts a little pressure on the steer to drive it into the pen, from a great enough distance that the animal isn't panicked into trying to escape by charging the partner blocking the hole.

As the steer walks quietly into the pen, the hole rider comes around and places her horse's head and neck in the gate to "hold" the steer and signal for time. The team's time was twenty-one seconds, and while it is not an award-winning time, this father-daughter team demonstrated perfectly coordinated teamwork in a nicely executed "training exercise" intended to educate the inexperienced horses they are riding.

Going for it.

One on One

This event has ten head of cattle and one rider. All the same rules apply; however, the "hole" between the pen and the wall will be covered with a panel. The single rider may not have more than two head of cattle across the halfway line and the time limit is one minute.

Team Sorting

There are ten head of cattle numbered zero through nine at the end of the arena. A team of three riders, once across the halfway line, will have a number called out. If the number is four, the team must sort the cattle, moving them across the halfway line, starting with the number four and moving up to five and so on until all ten are across the halfway line. If any of the cattle cross the halfway line out of numeric order or a previously sorted steer crosses back into the herd, the riders are disqualified. The time limit for this event is one and a half minutes. The team with the best time and most cattle sorted correctly wins.

This penner's "horse" is a mule!

A Preflight Check of Your Horse

Whether you are new to cattle events (or gymkhana) or are an old pro, certain elements are needed to ensure a good run. One of the most important elements is control. Can you be in control of your horse at all times? If you have ever been to a gymkhana or a cattle event, you have most likely witnessed at least one of the following problems: a horse and rider running erratically through the pattern, a horse who wouldn't stop running, pattern-marking equipment being knocked over as the horse ran into it, horses that refused to enter the arena, or horses that reared up once in the arena or in the roping box. All of these situations are signs of a horse out of control. The cause could be a number of things, including a horse and rider not equally matched; a saddle, a bridle, or a bit fit issue; a physical pain-related issue in the horse that is intensified by performance in the event; hooves that may be incorrectly trimmed and balanced, making the horse foot sore or lame; or a simple lack of training and confidence on the part of the horse.

Team Drafting

This event features three head of cattle and three riders. The object is to push the cattle through and around various objects and pen them at the end. The score is determined by fastest time (five minutes are allowed to move cattle around arena and obstacles), how many head of cattle went through the obstacles (there are one hundred total points, with points for each obstacle that each steer is navigated through), and how many cattle were penned. The first phase of the event is to move all three head of cattle around the perimeter of the arena in a controlled fashion, then drive the cattle around a cone, between two barrels, through a gate, and into the pen.

Glossary

bridle: A headpiece, usually made from leather straps, used on horses to control and guide them.

bit: A device, commonly made of metal, attached to a bridle and fitted into a horse's mouth.

body language: The primary language of horses, expressed through body positioning, gestures, and facial expressions, in order to communicate information.

chaps: Leather leggings of different designs and lengths originally worn to protect the rider's legs from brush, now a part of the standard western dress in western events.

cutting: A horse and rider separating a cow or a calf from its herd, then, without touching the animal, keeping it isolated against its will by out-maneuvering it in a head-to-head stand off.

doors: The various physical directions in which a horse can send his energy: front door equals forward, back door equals backward, and so on.

engaged: Refers to where the horse places his hind feet relative to the length of his body when in motion. Engagement of the hind leg affects the horse's balance point and his power potential.

English saddle: The English saddle differs from the western saddle in its much smaller size and its lack of a horn. It was designed and is used primarily for events that include jumping and dressage. *See also western saddle.*

FEI: The Federation Equestre Internationale is the worldwide organization that recognizes and governs horse sports, especially those contested at the Olympic level.

frame: The skeletal arrangement and use of specific muscle groups assumed naturally by the horse and/or demanded of the horse by the rider when in motion.

Gymkhana: A contest consisting of a variety of agility and obedience tests usually performed at speed.

hackamore: A bitless bridle.

halter: A piece of equipment loosely fitted to the horse's head to facilitate controlling the horse from the ground while leading or longeing.

hand: A term used to describe the height of a horse, measured from the ground to the top of the shoulder: one hand equals 4 inches.

headstall: The piece of the bridle that holds the bit in the horse's mouth.

hondo: The small loop at the end of a rope used to catch stock, through which the coils of the rope are threaded in order to form a loop for throwing.

jog: Both a speed and a foot movement pattern in a horse.

lead: The leading leg of a sequential footfall pattern of the horse's gait at either a lope or a gallop.

leg yield: A horse's action when he moves his body away from the pressure signal of a rider's leg in a forward, lateral moving direction.

lope: Both a specific speed and a sequential leg movement pattern in the horse. In order of speed, the gait names are walk, jog, lope, and gallop.

NRHA: The National Reining Horse Association is the governing organization for competitions in which the horse performs specific stylized patterns extrapolated from work the horse might be expected to perform when working with cattle.

on the bit: The state when a horse's energy is being delivered from the horse's engine (his haunches), willingly and without stiffness or tension, through his entire body into the rider's hands through the bit and reins. A state of lightness of movement, obtained through trust and correct body posture.

penner: Someone who participates in the discipline of team penning.

reiner: Term applied to either a horse or a rider who takes part in reining competitions.

reining: A western performance disciple demonstrating horse and rider skills, originally associated with working cattle in stylized patterns.

rollback: A physical action of the horse, requested by the rider, in which the horse quickly and dramatically changes his direction of travel by "swapping ends."

round pen: A physical structure of fencing material built in a circle designed to provide a place to contain and work a horse. The diameter of this type of arena varies from 45 to 70 feet.

saddle: A piece of equipment placed on the back of a horse, designed for both the security and the comfort of the rider. Usually made primarily of leather, it facilitates the rider's control of the horse. *See also English saddle; western saddle.*

saddletree: A frame, usually made out of wood, that supports the rider; it is the "skeleton" upon which a saddle is constructed.

seat bones: The two lowest points of the human pelvis, they are a part of the rider's communication system when mounted and the part of the human anatomy that should be positioned in the deepest part of the saddle just behind the horse's shoulders.

shoulder-in: A gymnastic exercise performed by the horse and directed by the rider, designed to increase the horse's suppleness and strength.

show pen: A popular term for a competition arena.

side pass: Descriptive term indicating a specific sideways movement of the horse. Also called *two tracking.*

sliding stop: A halt of all forward movement, accomplished by the horse when he engages his hind legs so far under his body that his hind end is lowered almost to a sitting position as he comes to a halt. In this movement, required in reining classes, the horse's hind feet leave long, even tracks in the footing.

spin: A 360-degree movement of the horse's front end around his stationary hind legs, usually repeated multiple times. It is a part of the pattern required in reining competitions.

stirrup: The part of the saddle where a rider's feet rest.

supple: The horse's ability to bend and give various parts of his body, both sideways and lengthwise.

team penning: Competition where the object of the contest is for team members to work together to round up cattle and move them from one place in an enclosed area into a small pen within the arena, holding them there until time is called.

TTEAM: Tellington-Jones Equine Awareness Method is a unique, highly effective, modern system of training horses.

turn on the forehand: An exercise where the horse moves his hindquarters in a circle around his stationary front feet at the request of his rider.

turn on the haunches: An exercise where the horse moves his forehand in a circle around his stationary hind feet at the request of his rider. Similar to a *spin*, but done at a much slower speed.

two tracking: Same as *side pass.*

western saddle: A type of saddle that includes a fixture on the front of the saddle called the horn, which provides a place for the rider to secure a rope, once it has been thrown over the neck or the feet of a cow or a calf. *See also English saddle.*

Index

About the Authors

Suzanne Drnec (Chapter 5)

Suzanne Drnec, president of Hobby Horse Clothing Company, designs and manufactures western show apparel. She describes herself as "born with the horse-loving gene!" Born in southern California in 1961, Suzanne remembers "living in the middle of an orange grove" with her mother, who granted her horse-loving daughter's dearest wish when she was just three years old: a Shetland pony as her Christmas present.

The salary of a sewing teacher didn't allow much of a budget for horse gear, so when Suzanne would ask for a blanket for her horse, her mother would suggest they try making it. It was from this experience that the seed of Hobby Horse Clothing and Catalog Company was to bloom.

"I started by making horse clothing and track room drapes. Then people began asking me to make custom clothes and show outfits. My first attempts at chaps were awful, so I ended up apprenticing with a superb chap maker who changed my life."

While the custom clothing business she started was creatively fulfilling, Suzanne recognized its profit potential was limited, so in 1991 she took the next step in her life, with the production of her first "Ready to Win" show apparel catalog. Today she continues to travel to major shows around the country, such as the Quarter Horse Congress, to find inspiration and see what really works in the show pen.

"What I think will work and what actually works are not always the same thing. Design is a creative, ongoing process and I always keep the goals of attractive, affordable, and comfortable in mind when I work," Suzanne says.

Her varied riding background, including showing hunters, reiners, Arabians, Paints, and quarter horses, undoubtedly stands her in good stead in the design studio. About horses she says, "I'm a sucker for a pretty face," Asked about any breed preference, she replies, "I'm sworn to fun, loyal to none."

Today Suzanne balances the roles of wife and mother of a toddler son with her busy life as a business executive and says, "I feel very fortunate to have been able to turn my horse hobby into my business. I never wanted to be a trainer, but my business still allows me to be around horses and horse people."

Nancy Cahill (Chapter 6)

Nancy Cahill grew up on the Texas coast where she spent most of her time on a boat with her father. But her proximity to the water didn't dampen her love of horses, which were on her mind twenty-four hours a day. Her mother, recognizing her daughter had all the signs of a serious addiction, arranged to take her daughter to Houston every week for English riding lessons. From that point on, the trail had all of the common landmarks of the "horse-crazy" child who becomes a "horse loving" professional equestrian. First it was lessons, then a horse, then another horse, and many after that.

While she was still in high school, Nancy started training horses professionally. While she has worked with a variety of breeds, the versatility and disposition of the quarter horse has made her a fan of the breed and influenced her career focus choices. She spent many years showing in both western and English disciplines, before deciding to specialize in the western classes due to their growing popularity. Since she was training horses for the public, teaching their owners how to ride those same horses became a natural expansion of her program. Many years of teaching skills to both horses and riders gave her what she considers a near perfect system of techniques that work on most horses and riders. As she experienced the great satisfaction of helping people learn how to work with and enjoy horses, the human teaching aspect of her business grew. While friends and colleagues have encouraged her to become a competition judge, with only so many hours in a day, she feels there is a greater need for teachers than there are for judges.

Nancy has been happily married to Bubba Cahill for thirty-one years and has two children, Quincy Cahill Allen and Cannon Cahill. Her daughter, Quincy, is a graduate of Texas A&M University and a six-time National Intercollegiate Champion as well as a World Champion in

Reining and Western Riding (winning the NRHA Intermediate Reining Futurity in 2004). Her son, Cannon, a golfer, will graduate from Texas A&M in 2006.

"My favorite horse so far is a horse named 'OK I'm Zipped,' who was a top ten Western Rider and Trail horse at the AQHA World Show for me and carried my daughter, Quincy, to wins at the Congress and a World Championship as well. He is everything a good horse should be: talented, pretty, quirky, and fun. I love horses! My philosophy on teaching, coaching, and showing, are all the same. It should be fun and safe. People can get satisfaction from any hobby, but a partnership with a horse brings something different to your life. You can take a problem kid and turn his life around with the help of a horse. The stresses of daily living or a tough job go away when an adult comes home and just hangs out with his horse. The horse industry is a little microcosm of the world and it is a great training ground. You can introduce a child into the world of horses and he will come out the other side with responsibility and make a better citizen."

Asked what she would change about the world she loves, Nancy answers, "If I had a magic wand, I would provide every horse owner with the knowledge of how simple it is to take good care of their horse economically and sensibly. Education is the answer to just about everything."

With a lifetime spent in the horse world, Nancy remarks on the changes she has seen: "The biggest change in the last twenty years is specialization. We breed horses for each event instead of for the all around individual. In one way, that has made for better horses in every event. On the negative side, we have lost some of the versatility that makes the QH such a great horse."

Besides her training and coaching duties, which usually include around twenty horses in permanent training, she also writes for such respected industry magazines as the *Quarter Horse Journal, Horse & Rider, Horse Illustrated, Performance Horseman, Progressive Farmer*, and *Western Horseman*. She has produced six videos on horse training, coached many youth and amateur world champions, and is a sought after guest on equestrian TV and radio shows. Her career credits include:

AQHA Reserve World Champ. Jr. Western Riding and Sr. Trail

AQHA World Champ. Jr. Trail and Jr. Western Riding

All American Congress Champion, in Western Riding

1988–2002 Coach of the Quarter Horse Youth World Cup Team

Founding member of the Texas Quarter Horse Assoc.

Youth Comm., and Halter and Performance Comm. AQHA Youth Comm.

2003–2004 TQHA Member of the Year

Clinician for AQHA judges seminars, Equine Affaire, Texas A&M, Georgia Horse Fair

Linda Morse (Chapter 7)

Linda Morse has made her living in the equestrian industry for thirty-three years. During that time, she has been what she terms a "general practitioner," working with riders in a variety of disciplines.

"My specialty was being very good at matching horses and riders," she says. It is a talent that has been proven over and over again, not only by the successes of her many competitive clients and their horses, but also by the enjoyment factor and safety record of her equally numerous noncompetitive horse and rider clients during those same years, a fact of which she is equally proud.

Starting her career as a western rider, riding stock horses under the great reining master, Monte Foreman, she also worked at the racetrack as a groom and an exercise rider; in the surgery theater of a large equine clinic; and rode herd and tended cattle on a 3,000-acre cattle ranch. During her professional career, she has started hundreds of young horses on their path as pleasure and performance horses. In the early 1990s, this strong, versatile horsewoman began living her ultimate dream when she purchased Brentwood Oaks Equestrian Center in Brentwood, California. Over the next eleven years, with her creative management vision and under her guiding hand, the center became an informational Mecca, as she organized, managed, and hosted multiple clinics for hundreds of horses and riders each year at the facility, bringing in a world-class roster of clinicians and instructors from all over the nation.

Although she has now sold her Brentwood Oaks facility, declaring herself semiretired, it is hard for a leopard to change its spots, so she continues to coach a few clients while she spends more time enjoying her second greatest passion in life, fishing, and begins a new adventure owning a marina.

Linda Huck (Chapter 8)

Linda was one of those little girls whose first word was horse. Growing up with cowboy and cowgirl figures like Roy Rogers and Dale Evans, she regularly imagined herself riding across a prairie or gathering cattle. Unfortunately, Linda grew up in Daly City, California. Her saving grace was that her home was a short distance away from a ranch located next to a huge livestock show facility known as the Cow Palace. The ranch had cattle, goats, and chickens, and, of course, horses, and she would do what ever it took to ride and be around the animals. After moving to Marin as a young adult, Linda always managed to have a friend or two who owned a horse. Linda picks up the story from here:

"The first horse I ever actually *owned*, an Arabian named Roban, who had successfully unloaded his owner enough times that she finally decided she could part with him, was a Christmas present from my husband. Needless to say it was the best Christmas present I ever received. I team penned, did gymkhanas, and rode trail on Roban. He was an awesome horse, athletic and agile, and I loved him dearly. Great love sets the stage for great tragedy, and so it turned out with Roban and I, when, one day, going out to retrieve him from the pasture for a ride, I found him with a broken leg.

"My next horses were both Arabians, both green broke—a gelding and a mare. The challenges I encountered training them led me to Tina Hutton, a system of horse training called TTEAM, and Centered Riding. Upon meeting Tina I realized I had finally found an instructor who taught principles of training and riding that made sense to me. Not only that, but implementing the techniques brought results with every horse!

"In feeding my interest in all things equine over the years, I have become certified in Equine Adjustments and Massage, Equine Sports Therapy and Hydrotherapy. Currently my husband, Bob, and I own Little Bit Ranch, in Emmett, Idaho, where I train horses and instruct riding. For many years I have felt the equine market place doesn't offer enough reliable mounts for children, so my long-term plan is to specialize in buying, training, and selling children's horses.

"Because many families whose child or children want to compete in High School Rodeo (where horses run barrels, do pole bending, team and breakaway roping, and even some jumping) often can't afford more than one horse, my training program focuses on creating all-around horses. Putting together a horse and rider team with the versatility to excel in all those skills is the challenge I most enjoy and the one that keeps me in the industry.

"My personal competitive history includes grand championships in gymkhanas and multiple wins in team penning and roping. One thing I always found to be true over the years: If you take good care of your horse, your horse will take good care of you."